MORMONISM, THE MATRIX AND ME

MORMONISM, the MATRIX and Me

My Journey from Kolob to Calvary

Tracy Tennant

RIGHT TRACK PUBLISHING
OLATHE, KANSAS

Right Track Publishing
P.O. Box 4712
Olathe, KS 66063
First Edition: March 2014
Second Printing: March 2015
Third Printing: September 2019
Printed in the United States of America
ISBN: 978-0-9913371-5-6
Library of Congress Control Number: 2014901100

Cover design by Carrol Schwabauer
Interior design and layout by Juanita Dix

*This book is dedicated to
those who value truth over tradition.*

I love it, love it, love it! This book is an intense walk through Tracy's life as she enters and exits a world known as Mormonism while eloquently comparing her story to the hit movie, "The Matrix." Her story will cause many to open their eyes to the world around them.

Tremayne Moore, *author of Deaf, Dumb, Blind & Stupid*

This book treats us to an engaging and insightful inside look at life in Mormonism, why people are leaving it, and the challenges in the journey to a new kind of faith. Tracy tells her story with sensitivity and humor in a way that Mormons and non-Mormons alike can appreciate.

Ross Anderson, *executive director, Utah Advance Ministries*

In her book Mormonism, the Matrix, and Me, Tracy Tennant details an inspiring account of God's amazing love and power, as well as His willingness to free those in bondage to error. Her story testifies to God's power to move heaven and earthm if necessary, to open the eyes of anyone desiring truth. This book gives hope to all who have loved ones trapped in false religion.

Tim Bonebrake, *pastor, Christ Family Church, Olathe, Kansas*

This book is a compelling "tell-it-all" story. After Tracy discovered solid historical evidence against Joseph Smith and teachings of the Mormon Church, she faced heart-breaking betrayal and rejection from her former Mormon friends and loved ones. However, knowing and understanding the real Jesus of the Bible has brought security and comfort to her heart.

Dennis & Rauni Higley, *H.I.S. (He is Savior) Ministries International*

Table of Contents

Acknowledgements

The inspiration for the title of my book came from Thelma "Granny" Geer's *Mormonism, Mama, and Me*, published in 1983 by Moody Press.

It's a Biblical imperative to give honor where it's due. There isn't enough room to list all the individuals who have made a difference in my life, so I'll name but a few.

I want to thank all the bishops I've had over the years: Bishop Aylesworth, Sagers, Folsum, Hall, Green, Nelson, Dinsmoore, Jepsen, Peterson, Smith, Herdt, and Lytle. There's probably half a dozen whose names I've forgotten, but for whom I had respect. Each of them was a man of good character and integrity. They taught me what it means to be a leader, to reach out to others, to serve tirelessly. Well, I'm sure they were very tired, but they served nonetheless.

To all the Relief Society presidents I ever had: Thank you for showing me what it's like to have compassion, charity, care, and concern for others. The countless meals you provided for ward members in need, the homemade bread and cookies you welcomed new families with, and the lessons you taught were inspirational examples to me. You helped me learn the importance of home and family, of being a wife and mother. You're amazing women whose shoes were too big for me to fill when I became Relief Society president.

To the many outstanding Latter-day Saints I've known in the Canoga Park 2nd, Pleasant View 2nd, University, 10th, Curtis Park, and San Miguel wards: I admire and respect you in so many ways. Thanks for special memories and fun times.

To the Crookston family, I give my unconditional love and gratitude. You taught me what family life is all about. Your examples of honesty, integrity, hard work, and commitment have been instrumental in shaping my life. You showed me (intentionally or not) that "mediocrity" is a dirty word; none of you was lukewarm about anything, especially matters of faith.

To Scott: Thank you for teaching me five new vocabulary words a week, a new joke every day, and how to have a sense of humor even in the direst of circumstances. God knows you taught me patience. Well, maybe not so much, seeing how things turned out. Thank you for your willingness to have lots of children. We almost made our "baker's dozen."

To my eight sons and two daughters: Thank you for being the awesome individuals you are! You have made my life exciting, rich, fulfilling, and fun. There has never been a dull moment being your mother. I love you so much and am proud of you beyond measure.

Special thanks to my mother, dad, Grammy, and Grampy (God rest their souls), and Aunt Al. You loved me, believed in me, supported me, and spoiled me rotten (as if that were possible), and taught me what it means to be passionately devoted to family.

Immense gratitude goes to my husband Greg. You got more than you bargained for. Thank you for loving me and my children, for taking care of us, for meeting our needs, for being a devoted husband and responsible father to some pretty strange people. I respect your desire to know God and His word, and your commitment to doing what is right and honorable. Thank you for putting up with me and my idiosyncrasies (which are aggravating at worst and endearing at best).

My gratitude to the many wonderful Christians who helped me after I left Mormonism. You encouraged me, taught me, befriended me, and demonstrated the love of God to me.

My Messianic Jewish friends and teachers; you have been mentors to me, and I'm so grateful that you showed me the beauty and value of the Tanakh and its teachings. You deepened my love, knowledge, and understanding of G-d and His ways.

Most of all, I thank Abba, my Heavenly Father, for His guiding hand that sustains me from day to day and for giving me Shalom—the peace that passes all understanding.

Foreword

Recently, there are many new books out about leaving Mormonism. I've been asked to comment on some of them, and I am humbled by the courage I see in these writers. Each has something new and important to say.

So, with so many autobiographical works on the same subject, do we need another? The answer is a resounding "Yes!" Tracy Tennant's realistic book is a look at not just LDS doctrine but LDS life. I've never read a book that so accurately—and sympathetically—looked at the challenges of trying to be a future goddess who'll rule worlds when your children's antics in church cause your fellow Mormons to leave services in a huff; or when the "spirit's leading" causes you to try to chase down your own car.

To be honest, at first I didn't feel I had time to read this book. I intended to skim over it, but ended up reading every word, savoring all the stories, laughing out loud over and over again.

The unique gift of this book—which may make it more apt to be read by a faithful Mormon woman than perhaps any other "ExMoBio" on the market—is its humor and vulnerability. Tracy doesn't represent herself as perfect, or even as a role model. I think she was as flabbergasted as the reader will be by the turns her life took. Her journey through Mormonism was costly to herself and even her closest relationships.

Call it gallows humor, if you will. But it is one of the funniest and most insightful books I've ever read.

Latayne C. Scott,
author of *The Mormon Mirage, Latter-day Cipher, Why We Left Mormonism, Why We Left a Cult,* and *After Mormonism, What?*

Preface

My purposes in writing this book is to give glory to God for leading me on an exciting adventure through life, an adventure with unexpected twists and turns as He brought me increasingly nearer to Himself and His truth. He is still leading me, revealing Himself through His word.

I hope to show those who eschew Mormons that Latter-day Saints are not caricatures of their religion. They are individuals with hopes and dreams, wanting only the best for themselves and their families. As a whole they aspire to do great things, to make a difference, and to live their beliefs according to the dictates of their own consciences without prejudice or reprisal.

As with any religion, you will find a wide range of personal beliefs and practices among members. Some adherents will be very devout and strictly follow the fundamental teachings of their leaders past and present, while others identify themselves as members in name only. Along that spectrum are individuals who believe *everything* their religion purports to be true, as well as those who only believe some of what it claims to be true. Thus, to pigeonhole all Mormons, ex-Mormons, Jews, Protestants, Catholics, Muslims—or any group for that matter—as being or believing a certain way is unfair and unwise.

I hope to show Mormons that those who leave the Church and speak out about its doctrines and practices should not all be vilified as mean-spirited anti-Mormons who, after being offended or too weak to "live the gospel," have some axe to grind under the influence of Satan. To the contrary, most of us leaving Mormonism do so for intellectually and spiritually honest reasons. We, too, aspire to do good, to make a difference, and to reach out to our LDS families and friends who are not acquainted with the troubling aspects of the Church, who might make different choices if only they had known. People have a right to know all the available facts about the group or organization they are a part of (or considering becoming a part of). This applies to all religious institutions.

To the detractors (Mormon apologists) who use the same old worn-out criticisms of those leaving the Church, and who accuse us of using "the same old worn-out arguments against Mormonism," let me say this: those arguments were not old and worn-out to *us*. They were new and fresh and raw and personally devastating. Perhaps *you've* been able to reconcile the discrepancies and problems in such a way as to maintain your belief in Mormonism, and if you value loyalty to the Church as paramount, then that's an issue between you and God. It's not my place to condemn your personal convictions. If you are being true to your beliefs, I can respect that. But I ask the same courtesy. Those of us who have left the Church were *not* able to reconcile the problems we saw in good conscience. We valued loyalty to spiritual integrity and intellectual honesty as paramount. To launch ad hominem attacks or dismiss our heartfelt concerns as irrelevant or trite is unfair, uncharitable, and unbecoming of someone claiming to be a representative of Christ and his church.

This book is more autobiographical than polemic in nature. Ideally, readers will be able to empathize and understand Mormon life better through the eyes of a mother of ten children who lived, breathed, and believed it wholeheartedly. Because the book is not meant to be an exhaustive treatment of the LDS religion, extensive references are not included. The references are best considered as starting points for those who are serious about engaging in further research.

This is *my* story, *my* experience with Mormonism. If you're LDS, some of my experiences may resonate with you and others will not. I'm not telling you what to believe. I'm just inviting you to share in my journey, and if you so choose, to examine your faith and see what it's founded on. You may decide you like things just as they are, or you might decide you want to know more before continuing on your path in Mormonism. It's *your* life, *your* eternal destiny to consider. No one can make that decision for you.

Theologically I can no more say that all self-identifying Mormons are going to hell than all self-identifying Christians are going to heaven. The matter of who is being redeemed and who is not is known to God alone. All I can state with assurance are the words of the Master, who warned, "If you do not trust that I AM [who I say I am], you will die in your sins" (John 8:24, *CJB*). It's imperative that we not only know *about* the Almighty, but that we *know* Him on a personal level.

Each of us—atheist or theist, regardless of religious affiliation—must decide who Jesus is based on the evidence. Is he merely a man or is he divine? Is he our older spirit-brother and brother of Lucifer or is he God incarnate? Did he progress to the status of godhood over time or was he always God (John 1:1)? Was he conceived by the power of the Holy Spirit or was he the literal physical offspring of God the Father? Is he the Messiah foretold by Hebrew prophets to establish the Kingdom of God on earth or is he an Exalted Being from Kolob sent to establish the Mormon Church? Did he come to reconcile man to God or did he come to make gods of men?

Whatever our conclusions, let them be based on the preponderance of evidence and not on feelings, spiritual experiences alone, or wishful thinking. Truth has nothing to hide. The truth will set us free.

Introduction

My choice would be as monumental as Neo's character's was in the 1999 movie *The Matrix*. I had the figurative red and blue pills placed before me, each carrying significant consequences no matter which one I chose. The movie's plot is that humans have become slaves under a system of Artificial Intelligence that keeps their minds blinded to reality by the Matrix, which generates a virtual reality for its victims. While people believe they're living as doctors, lawyers, businessmen, teachers, and more, in actuality they are hooked up to machines that use their bodies for fuel.

Neo must choose which path to follow. He can take the blue pill offered to him and "wake up in bed as if nothing had happened and believe whatever [he] wants to believe." Or he can take the red pill and be shown, like Alice in Wonderland, "how deep the rabbit hole goes." Neo carefully considers and chooses the red pill. His mind disconnects from the Matrix and he sees the world as it really is; a ravaged, desolate wasteland caused by a war fought between man and machine.

I contemplated the question posed by my husband Scott; "If the Church isn't true, would you want to know?" I thought about my life as a Mormon and how it encompassed every aspect of my being. All my decisions were based on the premise that Mormonism was the only true religion on the face of the earth, and no one could live in eternity with God unless he was a faithful member of *The Church of Jesus Christ of Latter-day Saints*.

"No," I answered, reaching for the blue pill. "I wouldn't want to know. It would be too scary. I mean, if Mormonism isn't true, what is? Even if it isn't, it's still the best thing out there."

Scott nodded in agreement. "Right, what other church teaches so many good things and is so family-oriented?"

That conversation became a benchmark for what followed over the months ahead; for what purpose does truth serve if it isn't sought after and followed? I came to understand that truth does matter, as it will either convict and condemn us or vindicate us and set us free.

In what discipline does truth *not* matter? The artist must understand basic truths about color; hue, value, and saturation. A composer must understand the elements of rhythm, melody, harmony, and texture to create musical order. Rocket scientists must understand the dynamics of propulsion, physics, and mathematics. Everything that means anything must be based on some type of truth or it can't function properly, if at all. Likewise, there are truths in the spiritual realm on which we must rely; truths which exist independent of our belief in them; bringing us back to the allegory of the Matrix.

As explained in the movie, "The Matrix is a computer-generated dream-world created to keep us under control, to turn us..." into a power source for advanced smart-machines. By way of analogy we can say a spiritual matrix exists; one that is demonically generated to keep us in the dark and turn us into fuel that feeds the very fires of hell. The Matrix is the system of spiritual deception used by the Enemy of our souls to keep us blinded to God's truth. It manifests itself through all worldviews not in harmony with biblical truth, be it atheism, humanism, polytheism, or aberrant theistic philosophies and religions.

In my case it was Mormonism that kept me from knowing the truth about the God of Abraham, Isaac, and Jacob; Jesus the Messiah; and redemption. This is my story, my testimony of how the Everlasting God brought me out of the kingdom of darkness into the kingdom of light.

CHAPTER 1

Zion, Here I Come!

The Matrix is everywhere. It is all around us; even now, in this very room. You can see it when you look out your window or when you turn on your television. You can feel it when you go to work... when you go to church... when you pay your taxes. It is the world that has been pulled over your eyes to blind you from the truth.

—Morpheus, The Matrix

I didn't see the telephone pole coming until it slammed into the front of my car. Actually there wasn't much damage, and it wouldn't have been so bad except for one minor detail; I had just turned sixteen and was taking the driving exam to get my license. I was trying to impress the test administrator with my amazingly skillful maneuvers while making a U-turn. Somehow the turn wasn't tight enough, and before I could hit the brake I hit the pole.

The humor of the situation struck me so profoundly that I could barely contain my laughter. Subdued chuckles burst from me every few minutes on the drive back to the Department of Motor Vehicles like geysers at Yosemite National Park. Surely the examiner would write this off as some freak incident recited from Murphy's Law of Teenage Disasters, like waking up on the day of junior prom with a zit bigger than the double-bacon-grease-burger you ate the night before or some other once-in-a-lifetime misfortune.

I kept glancing at the man, searching for any hint of a smile, but all I saw was his hands, white from gripping the seat belt too tightly, and a pained expression on his face that led me to believe he needed a bathroom fast! Being a keenly observant and astute young woman, I surmised that he wanted me to keep my eyes on the road. When we got back to the Department of Motor Vehicles' parking lot (and after he leapt from the car) I asked him with unabashed expectation if he was going to give me my license. He mustered up a polite smile and told me to come back when I knew how to drive.

Six months after finally getting my license I returned to the DMV, this time armed with a motorcycle belonging to a friend. I wanted to be as versatile as possible and get as many permits as I could. Weaving in between the little orange cones was no problem. Executing skillful and smooth turns was a breeze. Coming to complete stops at the proper markings in the test area was a flawless feat no less professional than what you would see at a police academy for training traffic officers. What presented a problem was driving in a straight line back to where the examiner was standing, at which time I side-swiped a parked car with my knee, resulting in a slow motion, sliding crash. The last thing I remembered was hearing my friend, David shouting, "Catch her! She's fainting!" and waking up on the hood of a random car.

It was reminiscent of what you'd find in a romance novel. Not the crash itself, but being swept up into the arms of the hero after you've fainted and being gently laid down on the hood of a car (a sports model no doubt) and waking up to gaze into the eyes of…the handsome hero? Not this time. The eyes I gazed into belonged to *the same guy who gave me my driving exam six months earlier!* That was not romantic; it was a nightmare! I'm sure visions of monster telephone poles flashed across his mind when my helmet was removed and he recognized my face. Clearly I didn't pass the test. After being assured that I would survive, he turned without a word and walked back inside, probably to arrange for his family to move out of state and away from any roads I might be driving on.

Eventually, I got my motorcycle permit and life in Utah continued to be a wonderful adventure. The move from Canoga Park, California eighteen months prior was exciting for my whole family, but especially for me. You see, I planned on marrying my Prince Charming, Donny Osmond, and living happily ever after. My heart was set on this teenage heartthrob, the seventh of nine children born to George and Olive Osmond. In my estimation Donny was the handsomest one of six performing brothers who made the Top Ten pop charts numerous times during the 1970's. The Donny Osmond dream didn't work out so well for me, but in time the "happily ever after" began the day I met my eternal king; the Prince of Peace. I guess I should start at the beginning.

I was raised by my mother, aunt, and maternal grandparents until my mom remarried when I was nine years old. As an only child I was precocious, spoiled, and curious about the world around me. Except for my baptism in a Methodist church and brief attendance at a Baptist Sunday school when I was quite young, I had very little formal religious training and was left to my own devices on how to find spiritual truth. Intrinsically I knew there was an All-Powerful God, but He seemed a little scary to me.

My mother bought me a book of Bible and faith stories with pencil-sketched illustrations in it. The drawing of Noah's Flood depicted terrified naked people crawling over each other to escape the rising waters. One story in the book told about a sick boy in the hospital who saw Jesus by his bedside before dying, which in my young mind meant if you see Jesus when you're sick, watch out! The couple of times I had been to a Catholic Church for a relative's wedding or confirmation, I saw a porcelain figure of a bruised, broken, and bloody Jesus hanging on a cross mounted to the wall of the sanctuary. Frankly, as a child with no understanding of these things, the pictures and stories frightened me.

I had a typical American upbringing. Although there was some alcohol, cigarettes, and occasional swearing in the home, I had no desire to do any of those things. I was loved and well cared for. My mother conscientiously sheltered me from the social chaos of the sixties and early seventies. I only became aware of the Vietnam War when I entered junior high school in 1972. Bumper stickers were as abundant as hip-huggers and bell-bottoms. Almost every locker had one plastered on the front reading "Bring Home our P.O.W.'S" or "God Bless the M.I.A.s."

It was 1974 when my best friend began asking me to attend the Mormon Church with her. Every Wednesday Liz would invite me to a mysterious meeting called "M.I.A." (*Mutual Improvement Association*).[1] I asked her what the acronym stood for and she didn't know. The only thing I knew was that M.I.A. meant *Missing in Action* and I wasn't about to go to some strange church meeting that used non-descript acronyms. Eventually though, common sense won out and when Liz invited me to a square dance at her church my love for dancing prompted me to accept the invitation. It was incredible! I felt like I was coming home. The people were warm and friendly, the kids my age were accepting and not driven by worldliness. The local Church of Jesus Christ of Latter-day Saints was an organization full of people just like me. It felt so wonderful to fit in.

When I got home from the dance that night, I excitedly told my mother I wanted to get baptized. She wisely advised me to wait until I knew more about the

Church, and no amount of pleading would change her mind. Disappointed, I said that all I wanted for my fourteenth birthday was to be baptized Mormon. Mom gave me permission to continue attending. I jumped into full church activity with my whole heart and soul, becoming the darling of the Canoga Park Second Ward.[2]

During the following four months I asked any adult in the ward who would listen all about the gospel. By the time my birthday approached I was considered a "dry Mormon."[3] Bishop Aylesworth informed me I was required to take the formal missionary discussions before my baptism. At that time there were seven official lessons which were taught once a week to prepare an "investigator" for baptism and membership in the Church.

The missionaries assigned to me were two young men about 19 and 21 years old. I was surprised they both had the same first names, Elder Peterson and Elder Backsendale, until they explained that "Elder" was a title. They taught me the basics of LDS doctrine; however, I kept plying them with questions about concepts I had heard at church, such as the Second Coming, the millennium, the New Jerusalem, getting one's "Calling and Election made sure," the white stone we're given in the next life, and other things I had heard about from Church members. Much to my dismay they insisted on sticking to the official lesson plans, stating they weren't supposed to teach me deeper doctrines. I had a voracious appetite for knowledge, but especially for spiritual knowledge. The elders advised me that I needed "the milk before the meat."

It meant so much to me to be "spiritually re-born" on the day I celebrated my physical birth that the Stake[4] changed their customary baptism schedule so I could be baptized on my birthday. My baptism was held on the sunny Saturday afternoon of my fourteenth birthday. About forty people were in attendance to see nine of us getting baptized; four children of record[5] and five converts. When everyone began singing the LDS hymn *The Spirit of God Like a Fire is Burning*, the air felt electrified to me, like angels had joined in the chorus to celebrate the occasion.

As a true-blue Latter-day Saint, I began to have longings to join the bulk of Church membership in Utah, which I equated with "Zion."[6] Particularly, I wanted to live in Provo, affectionately nicknamed Happy Valley by Church members. I recall a young man in my California ward being called to serve a mission in Provo, Utah. The whole congregation burst out laughing when the announcement was made over the pulpit because we all "knew" the only people living in Utah were Saints. Who was this poor boy going to proselytize, farm animals?

My family had grown weary of smog, crime, and traffic congestion, so in August of 1975 my grandparents and parents put their houses up for sale, and by the

end of September we were living in Zion! My dreams of Utah, meeting Donny Osmond, and living happily ever after were about to come to fruition, or so I thought.
I began attending Provo High School and set about making friends. Much to my
dismay, I noticed there was a difference between Utah Mormons and "mission
field" Mormons. Instead of finding everyone excited about living the gospel, it
seemed to me that many Utah Mormons were complacent about their faith.

Prior to moving, when my aunt and I took our first trip to Provo to see what
it was like and talk to a realtor, we drove to the Riviera Apartments on Canyon
Road to find the Osmond family. They owned the apartment complex and lived
on site to manage it. As soon as I walked into the office, George Osmond greeted
me warmly from behind the counter. I introduced myself, telling him my family
was thinking of moving to Provo from Canoga Park. I asked him where there was
a ward we could attend that Sunday and he invited us to visit the ward his family went to. Thus, after moving to Provo I began attending the Pleasant View 2nd
Ward in the Sharon East Stake, even though I lived outside the ward boundaries.

Every Sunday was a thrill, especially sitting as close to the front as possible,
hoping to catch Donny's eye as he sat at the Sacrament table.[7] Once in a while I
would be rewarded by his captivating smile. Gathering up all the courage I could
muster, I even invited Donny to a Girl's Choice dance being held at Provo High
School. To my surprise he smiled and said yes! Unfortunately, he had to break
our date a couple weeks before the dance because he was leaving town on tour.
Another chance to go out with him never arose, as Donny was often traveling with
his family. The opportunity for him to fall in love with me quickly evaporated, so
I decided to settle for a mere ordinary man. My first priority, however, was getting
my family to convert to Mormonism.

---

1. M.I.A. was the name of the LDS youth program at one time. Now it's just called the Young Men's
   and Young Women's programs. When I was a young teen in the 1970's we met on Wednesday
   nights, separating into various age groups to be taught a lesson or have an activity.
2. "Ward" is the term for an LDS congregation. Wards are determined by geographical boundaries set
   by the Church. Members attend the ward in which they are assigned, based on where they live.
3. "Dry Mormon" is a term applied to an un-baptized believer in Mormonism.
4. A Stake is a larger "precinct" or zone of church members. A stake is generally comprised of between five and ten wards.
5. "Children of record" or "Child of record" mean children who are born into LDS homes. This designa-
   tion applies before they receive baptism at the age of eight.
6. In Mormonism, Zion can mean "the pure in heart," as well as a specific place appointed by the Lord
   where his saints are to gather.
7. The Sacrament table is close to the front of the sanctuary. It holds trays containing bread and

water to be "blessed" (prayed over) by the priests (16 and 17 year old boys) and then passed out to the congregation by deacons (12 and 13 year old boys). Effective January 2019, boys will be ordained to the Aaronic Priesthood the calendar year they turn 12. Likewise, young men will be advanced to the priesthood offices of "teacher" and "priest" the years they turn 14 and 16.

CHAPTER 2

Competing for a Husband

I told you, honey, he may look like just another geek, but this here is all we got left...
—Anthony, The Matrix

My parents decided to take the missionary discussions because they thought it was a good idea to attend church together as a family. What a stir that created! A new "Gentile" in a predominantly Mormon neighborhood is like an uninitiated passerby who inadvertently wanders into an Amway convention. Ward members, neighbors, Home Teachers, Visiting Teachers, the Bishopric,[1] and a seemingly endless stream of missionaries descended on our home. *They* were excited! *I* was excited! It was a-dream-come-true for me to think I was going to have an eternal family.[2]

My parents were soon baptized and shortly afterward my dad had the Aaronic Priesthood[3] conferred upon him by the laying on of hands. Brother Bramer—one of our home teachers who lived next-door—came over almost daily for a couple of months. Often he came straight to our house from work before even going home. My mother thought it was because we always had fun at our house; playing board games and spending family time together. Brother Bramer sat and watched cartoons with my step-siblings and me, hung around during dinner, and tried to fellowship and friendship us every way he could. Finally, after he followed my friend and me into my bedroom (to join in whatever activity we were involved in), Mom told him it was time to leave and that he didn't need to come over any more except for official monthly home-teaching visits.

Soon after their baptisms, my parents were asked by the bishop to accept callings[4] and serve in the ward. It was too much too fast. Within six months they stopped going to church, quickly falling out of favor with ward members. The home teachers, Brother Wolfgram and Brother Bramer, stopped coming over. The neighbors stopped waving from their yards. The phone stopped ringing. Invitations to neighborhood events stopped being sent. And I stopped going to my mother for advice and sharing with her what was going on in my life because she just didn't know the "truth" of things. How could I expect someone who did not understand the gospel to give me advice about life? Instead, I began to confide in my ward youth leaders and the mothers of my LDS friends. My best friend from school became my advisor on boys and dating. I shut Mom out of my life. I idolized her when I was a child and we had always been very close, but now the Latter-day Saints became my new family. It broke my mother's heart.

I was oblivious to her pain, however, because my own heart was smitten with the Ray and Marvel Crookston family that attended the same ward as I did. They weren't rich or famous like the Osmond's, but they were well-respected in the community and committed to living the gospel. Brother and Sister Crookston had sixteen children; nine sons and seven daughters, because they took the teachings of Church leaders to not limit family size seriously.

"Hey, you want to go to a movie?" Scott looked at his watch. We had just finished rehearsing for a talent show being held at the Provo City Center. Several people suggested I ask Scott Crookston, a gifted musician and the ward organist, to accompany my singing on piano.

"That sounds fun," I said, wondering if this counted as a date. I decided it didn't, since the Church taught its youth not to date until they were 16. I was kind of excited and a little nervous because Scott was 23, eight years older than me. We looked at the movie page in the Provo Herald to see what was playing and settled on *Billy Long and the Traveling All Stars*. We stopped at Kentucky Fried Chicken on the way and picked up a couple two-piece meals to go. Scott insisted we could bring the food into the theater because he was one of the projectionists there and had special privileges. At least he *thought* he had special privileges. The manager pulled him aside a few days later and told him never to bring KFC in again. Apparently other patrons, after smelling the fried chicken, began bringing in their own meals and the concession stand was losing business.

When the movie was over Scott took me for a motorcycle ride. I asked him what would happen if we went over speed bumps at 50 mph. He replied, "I don't know. Let's find out," and soon we were flying over speed bumps in the near-vacant parking lot of the University Mall in Orem. Fortunately, we survived the foolhardy feat.

Scott and I became friends and often took long walks, talking about everything under the sun; the gospel, deep philosophical questions, relationships, science, and where technology was heading. Actually, Scott did most of the talking and I did most of the listening. He seemed to know so much, and what he didn't know he made up plausible explanations for. We read a book together that covered 13 goals a person should make in order to have a successful life. We started a tradition that lasted a little over a year. Once a week we walked to a little wooden bridge that went over a stream by a grove of trees near his house and pounded a nail into the handrail. Each nail represented a week of trying to achieve our goals.

"You know why it's so easy for us to talk?" Scott mused one day when we were on a walk. "It's because there's no chance we would ever marry each other, so there's no threat. We can be open without worrying about making an impression."

I nodded at his wisdom, though it wasn't long before I *did* want to marry him precisely *because* he was so easy to talk to. In contrast, Scott wasn't ready to marry anyone. About the same time Scott began dating me, he also began dating a young woman in the ward named Becky, who was closer to his age. Neither of us unsuspecting girls knew about the other until we were both head-over-heels in love. As you can imagine, two marriage-minded females vying for the same man made life miserable and painful for four long years. Scott couldn't make up his mind which one of us he wanted to spend eternity with or if he should look for someone else. He was afraid of making the wrong choice. He reasoned that if he said yes to one girl, he was theoretically turning down a million others.

Scott grew up being taught that the most important decision a person could make was choosing an eternal companion, so he was reluctant to decide. Becky was "Molly Mormon;" she cooked, cleaned, ground wheat, stored food, canned fruits and vegetables, was great at interior design, loved children, watched only "G-rated" movies, and was a great seamstress. It wouldn't have surprised me if she wove her own cloth from the hair on her legs. Scott really liked those qualities, especially for the stability factor. If he married Becky he would have a doting wife who was a good housekeeper. She would keep the children perfectly coiffed for Sacrament meeting; their sons in little homemade three-piece suits and ties, and their daughters in frilly dresses with ribbons in their hair. As ideal as that seemed, however, Scott was afraid his life would be extremely boring.

Scott imagined if he married me, life would be more of an adventure, plus—as he had made known more than once—my fully endowed, slender figure gave me an edge over the competition. If I fell short in the homemaking department, Scott could compensate in the eternities by adding a few wives to the mix through the New and Everlasting Covenant.[5]

Ambitious to become rich and famous, Scott and I got a couple gigs in Provo and Salt Lake City playing the piano and singing. About two years after we started dating we moved to Las Vegas to make the Big Time. I rented a room from a nice LDS woman, Ali Hafen, who became my "mom" away from home, while Scott rented a one-room shack with a bathroom in back of someone's house. A few months later Becky followed, unwilling to let the man she had invested so much time with fall into the clutches of a younger woman. It was more than irritating. She was a thorn in my side, as I was in hers.

I began attending a singles ward by the time I turned 18. Becky and Scott attended the University Ward next to the University of Nevada Las Vegas (UNLV) campus. Scott kept encouraging me to date other people, perhaps hoping I would find someone else, thus removing some of the pressure on him to choose a wife. At age 26, Scott was way past the normative age for LDS guys to get married. Returned missionaries, known as RM's, were encouraged to find a wife and settle down within a year or so of coming home from their two-year missions. Scott had been back for five years already, with no serious attempt on his part to find "the right one." Becky, 24, was practically an old maid according to Mormon tradition at the time. Her biological clock was ticking and she was vigorously pursuing Scott so she could go to the temple and be well on her way to securing an eternal family.

Oh, how I disliked her! One time Scott broke a date with me to go comfort Becky, who whined to him about being so mistreated by me at church when we all went to the same ward in Provo. Trying to be the better person, I smiled at her in the foyer. Immediately she went to Scott to report that I had "smirked" at her in passing. Such was the normal course of things during our four-year love triangle; Becky and I each running to Scott seeking justice over real or imagined hurts caused by the other.

I reluctantly went out on blind dates set up by Ali and even by Scott; but more often than not the guys were more interested in my bust size than my IQ. One guy had only been home from his mission for two days, and he had me cornered on the couch with his hand on my thigh at Ali's house. I indignantly told him to leave and literally planted my foot on his rear-end to push him out the door. I wondered why he told me on the phone to be sure to wear one of my designer tee shirts. That should have been my first clue (I worked at a small souvenir shop on Fremont Street called the "T-Shirtery," that specialized in personalizing tee-shirts, most of them rather tight).

Disillusioned after four years, Becky and I both got tired of waiting for Scott to make up his mind. Becky accepted an offer of marriage from an RM who started attending the University Ward after coming home. About a week later I accepted a proposal from someone who had his heart set on me for months, but at the time I wasn't ready to abandon the hope that Scott would one day be my husband. The young man was persistent, in contrast to Scott's indecisiveness. I decided it would be better to marry someone who was crazy about me than to take the chance of waiting for Scott to overcome his fear of commitment.

My engagement lasted a little over two months. "Albert" (not his real name) and I argued too much. He turned out to be very jealous and rather possessive. When Scott heard the engagement was off he asked me to come back, promising to work toward becoming temple-worthy so we could marry in the temple in a year's time. Surprisingly, his bishop counseled him not to wait, but to go ahead and marry me and get sealed in the temple a year later.

The very next week, Scott and I were married in Bishop Ashley Hall's home with my parents, aunt, Grammy, and half the ward in attendance. It was a lovely ceremony, prepared with only a day's notice. Thoughtful ward members made a wedding cake, fancy punch with ice cream sherbet and ginger ale, snacks, and even bought us wedding gifts. I'm thankful we had a civil marriage first or else my family—as non-members of the Church—would not have been able to be there in the temple to see their daughter get married.

We stayed in Las Vegas for our two-day honeymoon while Scott had the weekend off. Then life became serious business. We were "grown-ups" now, starting a family of our own with all its attendant responsibilities. I would work until children came along and then become a stay-at-home mother, as was a good Mormon woman's calling.

---

1. **The Bishopric** consists of the bishop (similar to a pastor) and two men called 1st and 2nd counselors who help the bishop in his function of leading the ward.
   Home teachers: Men in a ward are paired up with each other or with a 12 to 18 year old boy for the purpose of visiting ward members on a monthly basis. The home teachers are assigned a certain number of people or families to visit. They give a brief message from the First Presidency (the Prophet and his two counselors), published each month in the *Ensign Magazine*, and see if the

family has any special needs.

Visiting Teachers: Similar to home teachers. Each adult female ward member is assigned two visiting teachers (also females). Visiting teachers teach a brief lesson monthly to the ladies they visit and see if there are any needs. The visiting teaching program is also meant to strengthen relationships between women in the ward.

2. "Eternal family" in Mormonism means that the earthly family unit can continue intact into eternity (heaven) if all family members are "sealed together" (a type of ritual) in an LDS Temple and live out their lives in a worthy manner; keeping all the commandments and being faithful members of the church.

3. In Mormonism there are two levels or offices of the priesthood (or the authority to act in God's name); the first, or lesser one, is called the Aaronic Priesthood. When a boy turns 12, he is given this priesthood, which carries with it certain duties within the church. Male converts over the age of 12 are also given the Aaronic Priesthood first. Usually, when a young man turns 18 and is preparing to go on a mission, he advances to the Melchizedek, or higher office of the priesthood, for which there are other responsibilities.

4. Callings are essentially unpaid jobs in the church. For example, the bishop or one of his counselors might ask a ward member to accept a calling as Sunday school teacher or Boy Scout leader or to serve in some capacity in the Primary (children's ministry). Callings are said to be inspired by the Holy Ghost, so to turn down a calling is like turning down the Lord.

5. The New and Everlasting Covenant of marriage was foundationally the doctrine of plural marriage (or polygamy). Read *Doctrine & Covenants, Section 132.*

CHAPTER 3

Hidden Treasure

Did you know that the first Matrix was designed to be a perfect human world; where none suffered, where everyone would be happy? It was a disaster. No one would accept the program.

—Agent Smith, The Matrix

I walked in the door after work, glad to be home in the fading late afternoon, and flipped on the lights in our near windowless apartment. A dozen long brown cockroaches scattered, scuttling frantically across the kitchen counters to seek out the crannies from which they had come.

"Afternoon, Joe, Bob, Gertrude..." I called out their names. After all, the little buggers were roommates. Trying to evict them with several cans of bug spray and feebly attempting to lure them into "roach motels" had failed.

I flopped into a beige vinyl chair, the kind that come in cheap apartments, with brittle splits in the cushion and dust infested stuffing bulging through, and surveyed the task that lay before me. An hour until Scott came home and there was still dinner to make and the apartment to clean. That was unpleasant enough, but there in the middle of the living-room, large enough to have to step around, was Scott's "treasure." He would bring home his finds and, like a museum curator handling precious gems, carefully place a big pile of artifacts in the middle of the room to be sorted through at his leisure. He called it "neat things." I called it garbage. He said it was salvageable. I had a less complimentary word in mind.

Nevertheless, this ominous pile of "neat things" lay spread out before me in all of its glory. Some electronic parts, a crusty cake pan, a stereo speaker, and a stack of magazines with traces of coffee grounds and catsup on the edges. As a crown to the monument were some crumpled clothes and mismatched shoes that someone had thrown away. What if those red globs weren't catsup? What if the clothes had belonged to some murdered person or someone with a highly contagious disease such as jungle rot, and here they were on my clean living room floor spreading cooties? Well, I decided to clean around it and vowed to buy sterile gloves the next time I went shopping.

Messes straightened and dinner prepared, I awaited the arrival of my companion. He came home from work; my blue-eyed, fair-skinned hero, a shining knight in tarnished armor, and sat down with me to feast on Hamburger Helper. Those were the days when all I knew how to cook was prepared spaghetti sauce, Sloppy Joes from a can, and tacos. I would restart the cycle every three days unless I threw in Hamburger Helper for excitement.

"Dinner was good!" Scott burped. If we were from a less civilized country where a belch is a tribute to the meal, I would have felt honored. "Would you rub my back now? It's kind of sore."

Back rub? He got one three days ago. I know when we were dating I told him if he married me instead of The Other Woman I'd rub his back every day for the rest of my natural life, but that was the insane babbling of a desperate seventeen-year-old. I'd already forgotten that rash promise. Reluctantly, I acquiesced.

After my adept fingers performed an adagio dance up and down his spine, I sat down on our rock (the one disguised as a chair) and relaxed with a thrilling suspense novel while my husband carefully sorted through his treasure.

"Would you get me a glass of Kool-Aid?" Again an expectant glance was cast my way.

Just who did he think he was, anyway? We'd only been married a short time and already I'd been demoted to servant. *Well, sweetheart,* I thought, *the honeymoon is over.* We dated each other for four years and the "your-wish-is-my-command" romance took flight long before the "I Do's."

"Get it yourself," I countered.

"Oh, come on. Just get me some."

"No! I'm busy reading and you're just as capable of it as I am." My reprimand didn't faze him.

"Please? Just this once," he pleaded.

"Oh, all right," I sulked, going to the kitchen, slamming a cup down on the counter and opening the refrigerator door none-too-gently. Suddenly I felt very small. Sheepishly I looked at Scott and then back at the coral colored rose sitting in a delicate white vase in front of the drink pitcher. The precious card attached read "Happy Anniversary."

Maybe I *was* a tad unreasonable. "Do you really want something to drink?" I asked, giving Scott a big hug and a kiss.

"No. I just wanted to get you to open the refrigerator."

This time I got up, went back to the kitchen, and poured myself a glass of Kool-Aid to wash down the humble pie. I returned to my novel feeling less irritated about the pile of junk in the room. Scott continued to pick through the debris with a trash can nearby. The magazines with the red globs ended up in the "to-go" pile.

"Do you want this pan?" Scott held up an 8" x 8" cake pan with traces of petrified chocolate attached to the sides.

I viewed it with disdain and replied "No" somewhat forcefully. Besides, maybe it wasn't chocolate cake. Maybe it was dried blood crumbs.

"Look, you never know what you might find. I've brought home some pretty amazing things before," Scott chided.

My mind reflected on some of his more amazing discoveries. One time he found three twenty dollar bills laying in a trash can. It sure came in handy when we were behind on the electric bill. Another time he found a brand new pair of leather cowboy boots that fit his younger brother perfectly. Maybe this time there would be something we needed. If there was something valuable in Scott's excavations it could be the end of our Hamburger Helper days. Maybe we could afford to eat out every night, or better yet, hire a personal chef. I guess I could put up with a little mess if it meant finding a *real* treasure; old coins, valuable jewelry, a million dollars...

I was pulled out of my daydreaming by Scott's curious mumbling.

"Trace, look at this." He held up a package about the size of a hat box, wrapped in plain brown paper and taped all around the edges.

"What do you think it is?" I asked; my curiosity piqued.

Scott broke open the sealed portions of the paper. Sure enough, it was a hat box. There was duct tape and string circled several times around the box in all directions. Now I began to feel excited. I could tell Scott was excited too by his measured tone of voice, deliberately calm, stating that it was probably nothing. We both knew he didn't really think so.

"Get me the scissors," Scott directed. Greed was the only thing keeping me humble enough to obey instead of telling him to get them himself. I handed him scissors from the drawer, at least twenty years old with dull blades. They weren't too dull to get the job done though. Scott took off the lid, residue from the tape making it resist just slightly. Again another obstacle! Thick layers of cellophane encased the treasure.

"It's really heavy," Scott remarked.

"It must be very valuable," I observed, now giddy with anticipation. Money or gold coins; it had to be a large sum. Why else would it be so carefully wrapped? Maybe it was someone's life savings. My heart sunk at the thought. That meant we would have to turn it in and hope for a reward. But if it were ill-gotten gain, perhaps a pay-off from the Mob gone awry, we could keep it. Or if it belonged to a little old lady, like a childless widow, we could keep it. She probably died in her sleep in one of the apartments, a lone soul with no one to care for her. A maid must have cleaned the room in readiness for the next tenant and threw away all the widow's belongings as if they were tainted, oblivious to the treasure that was left behind. My imagination went wild.

Scott began peeling back the cellophane to uncover the contents of the box, so meticulously entombed, a golden mummy wrapped many times over in modern-day plastic bandages. Suddenly he shrieked as if bitten, dropping the bundle hastily.

"What!" I jumped. "What is it?"

"I don't know," Scott replied, somewhat shakily, "it looks like hair." He poked at the bundle lying at his feet and pulled back another layer of plastic-wrap. I could see a mass of dark hair and a deep crimson, almost black, thick liquid with tiny bubbles around the edges.

"Ooh gross!" My heart began to pound. I was right after all, about the clothes belonging to a murdered person, and a dismembered one at that. I was horrified by the prospect, but perversely pleased that I could say "I told you so." Scott picked back the plastic some more in macabre fascination to discover, not a severed head, but a dead cat. Someone's beloved pet that had been too precious to just toss in the garbage with cereal boxes and tomato sauce cans; someone's little friend that was given the best casket available. Scott had desecrated its grave. I straightened my back and shoulders. *I* would not be subject to any curse. *I* was not the one who had disturbed its resting place. *I* was just a curious on-looker.

Scott disposed of the body while I went back to reading my suspense novel. After scrubbing his hands thoroughly, Scott resumed sorting through his junk pile in search of treasure.

"Would you get me a glass of Kool-Aid?" Scott cast an expectant glance my way.

"Get it yourself," I answered without looking up and *this* time I meant it. I really didn't feel like getting up anyway. Strange things were happening inside my body.

CHAPTER 4

Preparing for the Temple

The Matrix is a system, Neo. That system is our enemy. But when you're inside, you look around, what do you see? Business men, teachers, lawyers, carpenters. . . . You have to understand, most of these people are not ready to be unplugged. And many of them are so inured, so hopelessly dependent on the system that they will fight to protect it.

—Morpheus, The Matrix

I had morning sickness that lasted till night and always felt on the verge of retching. Drained by all the changes going on in my body, I slept fifteen hours a day. I was angry with Heavenly Father for ordaining women to suffer in pregnancy and childbirth. Men seemed to get away with everything. They had it so easy and got to hold the priesthood besides. It just wasn't fair. To make matters worse, the thought of having to live throughout eternity vying with a dozen or more other wives for Scott's affection did not improve my mood any.

I could only imagine (and often did) what it would be like to have Scott leave several nights a week to make love with his other wives. I'd been informed by one LDS Institute teacher[1] that when the Scripture said there would be a "restitution of all things" during the millennial reign of Christ, it included plural marriage. As distasteful as plural marriage would be, I would just have to accept it or else face the fate Emma Smith was threatened with if she did not accept her husband Joseph's additional wives;

> And I command mine handmaid, Emma Smith, to abide and
> cleave unto my servant Joseph, and to none else. But if she will not
> abide this commandment she shall be destroyed, saith the Lord;
> for I am the Lord thy God, and will destroy her if she abide not in
> my law (Doctrine and Covenants 132:52).

My experience with Becky had been a painful one. If that was even a slight foretaste of what polygamy would be like, I couldn't imagine in my worst nightmares what it would be like to live like that for all eternity. What sorrow, heartache, and loneliness would come from only seeing my husband once a week, month, or year, depending on how many goddess wives he would have. Scott would hardly ever be home in our heavenly mansion. I wanted no part of it; yet, if I could not go to the highest degree of the Celestial Kingdom[2] without allowing for numerous "sister-wives," then I guess I would have to adjust somehow.

Regardless of how many wives Scott would have in the eternities, the first step for either of us on our path to eternal progression[3] was to be sealed in the temple for time and all eternity. We strove diligently to prepare for the special event. I hoped that neither of us would die before we got to the temple, lest we spend an eternity apart from each other. I wanted to be righteous enough to be an eternal family and daily lived so as to be worthy of the blessings of the temple. We went through a temple-preparation class and eagerly looked forward to being sealed together.

My husband and in-laws had forewarned me that the endowment session was somewhat unusual and that some people feel uncomfortable the first few times going through. Scott took out his own endowments before his mission and told me as much about the ceremony as he could without violating the sacred oaths he had made. I was told that what went on in the temple was "sacred, not secret," but the reality was we were not to reveal to anyone beyond general terms what went on inside; hence, secret.

After attending a series of preparation classes, I felt ready and excited to finally be going to the temple. We were interviewed individually by our bishop, followed by a second interview with the stake president. They asked questions to determine our worthiness to enter the temple. We had to have firm testimonies of the "Restored Gospel." They asked if we "sustained the President of The Church of Jesus Christ of Latter-day Saints as the prophet, seer, and revelator" and if we recognized him "as the only person on the earth authorized to exercise all priesthood keys." We were asked about our chastity, honesty, and whether or not we were full tithe-payers. They wanted to know if we "affiliate[d] with any group or individual whose teachings or practices [were] contrary to or oppose[d] those accepted by The Church of Jesus Christ of Latter-day Saints," or if we "sympathize[d] with the precepts of any such group or individual." Did we keep the Word of Wisdom?[4] Among other questions, we were finally asked if we considered ourselves "worthy in every way to enter the temple and participate in temple ordinances." Once we passed the interviews, we received our "temple recommend;" a wallet-sized slip of paper signed by the bishop and stake president, validating our worthiness to enter the House of the Lord.

The much-anticipated time arrived. One year and a day after our civil marriage ceremony, I took out my endowments in the Salt Lake Temple so that I could go through a "live session" (with live actors, instead of the movie). We were seated across the room from each other—women on the left, men on the right—with about 80 other people going through the session. The Mormons in attendance came from all walks of life; doctors, lawyers, carpenters, businessmen, mechanics, teachers, nurses, homemakers, grandparents, and home-schooling moms. Regardless of status, the playing field was leveled when we all dressed in white and waited for further instruction to progress toward godhood.

The following day we were sealed for eternity in the Provo Temple, along with our infant son. The temple workers dressed Quinn in an all-white creeper, white socks, and soft white booties with pom-poms. He looked like a tiny cherub depicted on a Hallmark greeting card, gazing intently at the man performing the ceremony as if he understood every word.

Even though I anticipated some unusual things about the endowment ceremony,[5] I was troubled by the blood oaths (we covenanted to suffer our lives to be taken in gruesome ways rather than reveal the signs and tokens to anyone) and wondered why we needed to learn special signs and tokens anyway to pass by the angels to get into the Celestial Kingdom. Did that mean if an outsider found out what these signs and tokens were that he could sneak into heaven? Would an omniscient God really need these tokens and our "new name" in order to recognize us? Why did all the women, and likewise all the men, get the same name on any given day? In other words, all women going through the temple on a particular day might be given the special name of "Rachel," while all the men might receive the name "Peter." I thought each person would be given a special and unique name, known only to oneself and to the Lord.

In one portion of the live enactment (and also in the movie version played in other temples) a Christian minister was portrayed as a hireling of Satan who taught a strange concept of God. Apparently, according to the script, Christians believed in "a God who is without body, parts, and passions; who sits on top of a topless throne; whose center is everywhere and whose circumference is nowhere; who fills the universe, and yet is so small that he can dwell in your heart; who is surrounded by myriads of beings who have been saved by grace, not for any act of theirs, but by his good pleasure." Like the character of Adam in the temple reenactment, I, too, could not comprehend such a Being, and was thankful to know that God was really an exalted human; someone I could identify with and become like.

We were taught certain hand-clasps and key words that would "enable [us] to walk back to the presence of the Father, passing by the angels who stand as sentinels, being enabled to give them the key words, the signs and tokens, pertaining to the Holy Priesthood, and gain [our] eternal exaltation."[6]

We were warned in both words and implied violence that violating the sacred obligations taken upon ourselves in the temple would bring the judgment of God upon us. It was hard to understand why our eternal destination would be jeopardized if we revealed to others what went on inside the temple. The thought certainly carried an element of fear with it, but we set all our questions aside and dedicated ourselves to faithful temple attendance, forging ahead in our efforts to rear a righteous family.

---

1. **LDS Institute** is the college-level counterpart to youth seminary. Mormon **seminary** is a CES (Church Education System) program for youth in grades 9 – 12. LDS teens attend for about an hour each morning before school starts; unless it's in Utah, where kids can attend during the school day on "release time." Non-Utah students usually go to seminary at a stake center near the high school, but in Utah (at least in Provo) the seminary building was adjacent to the public high school.
2. Mormonism teaches there are three heavenly kingdoms that people will be assigned to after the Judgment; Telestial, Terrestrial, and Celestial.
   Telestial Kingdom: This is considered the lowest level of glory where liars, murderers, adulterers, thieves and such go, after paying for their own sins for a thousand years in a temporary "hell" during the millennial reign of Christ on the earth. So, even Hitler, Stalin, Mussolini, and the vilest of persons will eventually get to dwell in a level of glory forever. People in the Telestial Kingdom will be ministered to by the Holy Ghost.
   Terrestrial Kingdom: This is the middle kingdom of glory, where the "good people" of the earth will dwell forever. This includes Christians and lukewarm Mormons. People in the Terrestrial Kingdom will be ministered to and visited by Jesus Christ.
   Celestial Kingdom: This is the highest of the three heavenly kingdoms where faithful, Temple-worthy Mormons will go. They become heirs of all God has to offer. Within the Celestial Kingdom are different degrees of glory. Only those who have been sealed (married) in the Temple can reach the highest level. They will have the opportunity to be married for all eternity, conceive and have spirit children, and become gods of their own worlds. They will be able to live in the presence of the Father and the Son.
3. **Eternal progression** is the path a Mormon advances along toward godhood.
4. **The Word of Wisdom** is the dietary laws found in D&C (Doctrine and Covenants) section 89. The main instruction is for church members to avoid hot drinks (considered to be tea and coffee; al-

though herbal tea is okay), tobacco and alcohol, and that meat should be eaten sparingly; only "in times of winter, cold, or famine" (most LDS ignore this part).

5. One of four main rituals or ordinances performed in LDS Temples. These four are: vicarious baptisms in behalf of the dead, initiatory, the endowment, and sealings.

6. John Widstoe, *Discourses of Brigham Young*. (Salt Lake City, Deseret Book Company, 1941), 146.

CHAPTER 5

Motorcycle Mama

Haven't you learned by now, that it is impossible to understand why they do the things they do?
—Agent Smith, The Matrix

The contractions were coming pretty regularly, so we hopped onto our motorcycle to see the midwife. After our station wagon finally gave up the ghost, we couldn't afford to replace it. For a whole year all we had was a motorcycle. The midwife checked how far along in labor I was and said we probably had a couple of hours to go. Rather than wait around we went to a nearby shopping mall. I needed a new nursing bra and was given extremely fast service by the department store clerk. I suppose she was concerned that I would deliver right there in the lingerie department.

This was our third child and the first time I would be delivering in a hospital. We had gone to a birthing clinic to deliver our first two babies because we didn't have medical insurance. This time Scott worked for an employer that offered benefits. No more natural childbirth for me! Leave natural childbirth to the kangaroos and koalas where a tiny one-inch embryo crawls up its mother's belly and climbs into a pouch. I think I could stand that. One day you're bending over to tie your shoes and voilà; out drops a little embryo. Then you just stick it in your pouch and take it out nine months later when you see a little hand poking out and waving hello. When Scott and I created our own worlds in the future, I planned on looking into kangaroo-like human births. The fact remained that women had to give birth the hard way, but I would do what I could to alleviate the pain. Now that I was in a hospital all I had to do was kick back and let the epidural take effect. It was slightly alarming to feel the anesthesiologist screwing something into my spine—at least that's what it felt like—but when I could no longer feel the painful contractions it was pure bliss.

Scott was hungry after waiting with me in the hospital for four hours and wanted to grab a bite to eat. The nurse checked me and said that I was six centimeters dilated, and there was plenty of time for him to grab dinner and come back. With two quick deliveries behind me I was somewhat doubtful, but reluctantly let Scott go with the admonition to hurry. Only minutes after he was gone the epidural wore off. To go from zero pain to full throttle was quite a shock, and to top it off it felt like the baby was coming. Calling out to the nurse, I told her I felt like pushing. She rolled her eyes with a patronizing kind of look that communicated the message, "I'm the expert and you're just an ignorant patient. Surely a woman doesn't go from six to ten centimeters in a matter of minutes, so please don't waste my time;" *that* kind of look. But she checked anyway just to humor me and found that I was right. I was dilated to ten and the baby's head was crowning.

How a person could move so slow and still be alive is beyond me, but with a snail-like pace she moseyed down the hall pulling the gurney behind her toward the delivery room. If you're a mom, you know how it is when you're in labor; I could count the colored tile squares on the floor by the wheels going from black to white to black. Driving to the hospital in labor is no different; every bump sends you into orbit. "We just went over a crosswalk, didn't we honey? Can you take it a little slower going over the paint on the road?"

Less than ten minutes after my husband left for Kentucky Fried Chicken, we had another son. Scott was still licking his fingers when he returned to find he had missed the most awesome experience in the world: the miraculous birth of another human being. It was hard to believe we now had three boys.

At the nurse's urging I decided to stay overnight to "get some rest." Besides being disturbed every hour to have my blood pressure taken, the new nurse coming on shift woke me up at one a.m. to introduce herself (Pow! Zoom). Then at five a.m. another nurse woke me up to give me a laxative, as if waiting three more hours would have meant a lifetime of constipation. I vowed never again to spend the night at a hospital for rest if I had any say over the matter.

The morning after Tristan was born we found out that we weren't covered by insurance after all. Hospital personnel had somehow overlooked verifying our coverage, and we learned that the president of the company Scott worked for had declared bankruptcy and was pocketing our insurance premiums over the past several months. We packed our things and asked to be discharged. Our baby had to stay a few more days due to a low Apgar score (newborn assessment). Hospital policy stated that patients were to be taken out to their cars via wheelchair, and we were asked while signing the paperwork what make our vehicle was.

"Kawasaki 400," we replied.

The desk nurse was incredulous. "You mean you plan to leave on a motorcycle?"

"Yes. That's how we came here."

"I can't release you to a motorcycle."

"Then release me to the bus. It goes right by our house" (a slight exaggeration). Back and forth we went offering solutions and presenting arguments, but she wouldn't budge. She said the hospital had a special fund and would pay for a taxi to take us home, but the truth was I had a dental appointment that I forgot to cancel and besides, I saw no reason why we had to take a taxi when a motorcycle would do just fine. The nurse was adamant about not letting us leave. Scott, who was not very assertive, surprised me by looking sternly at the nurse and saying, "You have two minutes to sign the release or I'm taking my wife and leaving."

"Oh dear!" the nurse mumbled, throwing in a few expletives. "Then I'll have to get my supervisor." She trotted off down the hall, and two minutes later Scott's watch alarm went off. "It's been two minutes, let's go."

"But what if we get in trouble?" I protested.

"What can they do?"

"Well, what if they don't give us our baby back?" I was suddenly worried.

"They can't keep our baby just because we don't have a car." Scott's assurance gave me some comfort, so without waiting any longer we quickly walked down the hall, out the door, and made a mad dash for the parking lot (actually it was a slow dash on my part). We hopped on the motorcycle (actually it was less of a hop and more like a slow climb on my part) and rode to the dentist's office to get a cavity filled (cavity in my tooth; not the one left by the baby).

"And how are you today, Tracy?" the dentist asked, probing my mouth with some medieval-looking instrument.

"Oh, a little tired and sore," I replied as best as I could with what seemed like both his hands in my mouth. He raised his eyebrows, and I explained that we had just come straight from the hospital delivering a baby and didn't want to cancel my appointment on such short notice. Over the ensuing years my fame went before me. Dental hygienists whom I'd never even met knew me as the motorcycle-baby-lady who came in for a filling.

A few days later my new visiting teacher took me to the hospital in her car to retrieve my baby who was ready to come home. Soon, my visiting teacher and I became very close friends. One day I saw her with a bruise on her face and she revealed to me that her husband, who was secretary in the bishopric at the time, frequently hit her. I wondered how it could be that the bishop called someone to a leadership position without knowing from the Spirit he was unworthy.

Over the following year "Terry" and I really bonded and became a great support to one another. She had a physically abusive husband, and I had woes of my own, though not nearly as bad. Still, family life became increasingly challenging as financial problems stacked up. Terry needed money to file for divorce, and I needed money to keep our first home from going into foreclosure. Financial stress was beginning to take its toll. Scott was working two jobs, and I was left to be both mother and father to our little ones in his absence.

I had another good friend in the ward that had children the same ages as mine. We met at a "Young Married Adult" activity at church and found we had much in common. LeAnne's husband was overworked and underpaid, so she decided to go to school to get a college degree. She encouraged me to get my G.E.D. and an associate's degree. Even though I did well in grade school and junior high, my high school education took a nosedive. I found socializing and dating Scott to be much more interesting than my classes, and consequently left high school only one quarter credit short of graduating. I'd regretted it ever since. LeAnne was certain I would do well. Between the three of us, we were able to watch each other's kids while Terry worked and LeAnne and I attended the local community college on grants and scholarships.

It wasn't too long before I gave birth to our fourth child; our first girl. It wasn't a planned pregnancy, but Scott and I agreed we wouldn't limit our family size. There were spirits waiting to be born into our home. Still, I wasn't ready to be pregnant again. I was overwhelmed with raising our three boys and going to school more than full time, pulling 20 credits a semester (later graduating on the Dean's honor roll), and hoping we didn't sink financially.

That year, the First Presidency announced during General Conference that a temple was going to be built in Las Vegas. Each family in the stake was challenged to pledge a certain amount toward the temple fund. Scott and I were asked if we could give $1,000 over the next year, which was well beyond our ability, but we had faith the Lord would help us.

To top off all that pressure, it was left up to me to go to church alone with all four kids each week while Scott worked. It was bad enough having a husband who worked on Sundays, let alone one who worked in a casino.[1] At least his job didn't involve gaming or alcohol, in which case he wouldn't have been able to hold a temple recommend. Sunday became the worst day of the week for me. I'd struggle to get the kids out of bed, change diapers, prepare the diaper bag, get dressed up, clean up messes, and change the kids' clothes a second time after somebody spilled something on himself and someone else.

By this time we had a car again, so I'd load all the kids up, get them strapped into their car seats, get to church ten minutes late (Mormon Standard Time) and then stumble into the sanctuary with a baby carrier in one hand, a toddler on my hip, and a preschooler hanging on each leg, while balancing on high heels and trying not to knock people over.

LeAnne conducted the music for Sacrament Meeting, while her husband Carl, and their three little girls, shared a pew with us. Invariably, Carl would have to take their crying infant out to the foyer, leaving me with his rambunctious daughters and my own lively crew.

One Sunday I sat in the chapel with LeAnne's children and my own. They were actually behaving better than usual, in my opinion. No one was rolling under the bench, running down the aisle, fighting over coloring books, choking on Cheerios, or hurling Legos through the air. The kids were a little restless, but certainly no more than any of the other children scattered throughout the congregation. Sixteen-year-old priests recited prayers over the Sacrament bread and water, after which twelve-year-old deacons began passing the Sacrament along the rows of people.

Suddenly, Sister Shields—whose husband had been the previous bishop and was sitting behind me—stood up, put her hands on her hips, and broke the near-silence by loudly exclaiming, "Well! I'm not taking any more of this!"

"This" was in reference to my restless brood. All eyes turned upon her and then me. I was absolutely devastated and humiliated. As quickly as possible I gathered up my children and our belongings and left the chapel sobbing. I was never coming back. Not ever.

---

1. The Church has since changed its policy. There was a time when church members could not get a temple recommend if they worked as cocktail waitresses, dealers, or on the gaming floor; although, ironically, it was okay for a person to be in an administrative position in a casino and have

a temple recommend. If gambling is "of the devil," then shouldn't any type of association with the gambling industry be unbecoming of a Latter-day Saint?

CHAPTER 6

Petunias and Pepper Spray

There's no point in worrying. Whatever is going to happen is going to happen.

—Trinity, The Matrix

I was still crying when we arrived home, and cried on and off throughout the rest of day. How could I ever face the ward again? Couldn't people see I needed help handling all my little ones with no husband there? One man in the ward, Brother Migrant with six kids of his own, occasionally sat with my boys when I had to take the baby into the foyer. He was the only person who actually helped instead of giving me irritated stares.

By the next morning I had calmed down enough to think things through. I realized whatever decision I made would be pivotal. If I didn't go back to church, what example would that be setting for my children? If I stayed home on Sundays until Scott could change his work schedule, what were the chances I would just become inactive and not return at all? What was more important; what Heavenly Father thought of me or what people thought of me? If I stopped attending church because of embarrassment I would be affecting future genera-tions. When looking at the situation from that perspective I saw that I had no choice but to do the right thing and continue going to Sacrament Meeting.

I was now left with the task of reconciling my relationship with Sister Shields. I got a pretty card and wrote her an apology, essentially saying I recognize she comes to church to be edified and expects a peaceful service without distractions, and how sorry I was that my energetic brood disrupted her. I explained how difficult it was for me to take the kids to church without Scott there to help, but how I wanted to do the right thing by bringing them. I told her how much I respected her for raising such a wonderful family and that maybe, as a seasoned mother and grandmother, she could give me some advice on how to improve. I dropped the card in the mail so she would get it before Sunday, and prayed that Sister Shields would be mollified.

On Sunday I got the family to church early enough to find a seat in the back. Normally the back pews fill up first, leaving only the front few rows available for latecomers. I was dismayed that Sister Shields didn't come that day and hoped we hadn't chased her off. She missed church the next several weeks, but at Stake Conference Bishop Shields came up to me, put his arm around my shoulder, and thanked me for sending his wife that card. He said she was truly touched by it. He told me she had been under stress in their family-owned business and he was thankful I reached out to her like I did. Even though peace was made with the Shields', I looked forward to moving out of the ward.

We had quickly outgrown our two-bedroom house and decided we needed to find something bigger. Considering the thirty-something other houses for sale in the neighborhood, some of which had been listed for over a year during a housing slump, we decided to sell it ourselves, asking for a very low down payment to assume our mortgage. We chained the kids to the peach tree (at least we would have liked to) to keep their little mitts away from the walls we just painted and wallpapered. We hosed down the stucco and scrubbed the windows and doors. Our children, who were quite rambunctious anyway, turned into a snarling, slobbering demolition crew when they found out that Mommy and Daddy were especially anxious that the house be kept spotless. It seemed as though their fingers turned colors and the word "Crayola" appeared over every knuckle as they ran their hands along the walls. They galloped through the house with carpet-snagging spurs that mysteriously grew out of their heels. Dirty fingerprints fell from their fingertips like autumn leaves falling from trees.

Potential buyers came with anticipation written all over their faces, only to run from the house in horror after viewing the clutter and chaos. Suddenly every speck of dust loomed before my eyes as if it were a mountain of dirt. There were no longer barely-noticeable spots on the carpet; the whole carpet itself seemed like one giant stain. I cringed in shame before every scrutinizing eyeball that passed through our doors.

Desperately I tried to interest everyone in buying our little house, even making comical promises. After a few weeks, a man who had already seen the house called back to say he wanted to buy it. "Now," he asked, "did you say the moon would be coming UPS or Federal Express?" I explained he was already getting a great deal on a silver platter, but I would have a hard time delivering the moon after all. He bought the house anyway.

Our friends, the Hammer's, offered to let us stay with them in their mobile home until we could find a bigger house. It was a pleasant looking trailer park with well-kept yards. After a few days our five-year-old son, Jeff, discovered that the front of the trailer across the way was made to look like the bow of a ship with pretty flowers in it trailing over the side. "Well," he must have thought, "it would be fun to sit in the bow of a ship and pretend to go sailing!" So, he proceeded to climb onto the "bow of the ship" and sit on the fastidious neighbor's petunias. Later that afternoon she came over very irate (understandably so) about her flattened flowers. I apologized profusely, thinking that it would be a nice gesture on my part, as well as the right thing to do, to replace her flowers.

The following day was Sunday, and while we were at church someone turned off the water valve in this woman's front yard. She assumed it must have been one of my children and stormed over to cuss me out. I tried to explain that we were we gone all morning, and the children were inside all afternoon. We didn't let them play outdoors on Sundays. She wouldn't listen. Between expletives she threatened to go to the manager. Following through with her threat, she filed two complaints against us. What a welcome to the neighborhood. I was planning to replace her flowers, but after she reported us there was no way I wanted to do her any favors. She got her reward, I reasoned. Why should I do something nice after suffering all that verbal abuse?

The manager came over that evening to ask when we were planning to leave. She gave us three weeks to be out of our friend's home. I did *not* have the best of feelings toward LeAnne's neighbor. The more I thought about it, the angrier I got. Over the rest of our stay I lost sleep over the incident. At night I lied in bed fantasizing about sneaking into her yard and pulverizing the rest of her petunias and doing a little begonia bashing as well. Of course, I couldn't really follow through with that, so I thought about leaving her a note instead, telling her exactly what I thought of her. I did nothing but feel bad until we moved three weeks later.

My unkind thoughts were consuming me, so I prayed for the bad feelings to be taken away because they were cankering my soul. After praying, the bitterness left me. I no longer had hard feelings, but neither did I feel love for my temporary neighbor. Still, I realized I needed to do what was right and buy her some new flowers to replace the ones that got crushed beneath Jeff's wiggly bottom. As I was looking at plants at the local nursery, a feeling of excitement came over me. Instead of choosing something cheap to placate the woman, I picked out the prettiest flowers I could find, even though they were more expensive. I wrote her a note giving her the benefit of the doubt, stating that I wished we had met under different circumstances because I was sure she would be a worthwhile friend to have. Quietly, I left the flowers and note card on her porch. A few days later LeAnne called to say that this woman came over to apologize. She was very touched that I replaced her flowers and left her a kind note. The great lesson for me in that experience was that action precedes emotion. I was beginning to learn some valuable lessons in human relations.

We found a small four-bedroom house, still in the North Stake, and were excited to begin a new chapter in our lives in the new ward. There were several LDS families living on our street. One family lived directly across from us, another two doors down, and one on the corner. The best part was that the church was right across the street at the end of the block. It wasn't long before we were given new callings. Scott was asked to teach in the Primary, and he became one of the ward's organists. I was made den leader over the Cub Scouts and in-service leader for the Primary teachers. We joined the choir; Scott as a tenor and me as an alto.

Our choir director, Bruce Green, was brilliant and talented. He also directed a prestigious local LDS choir, the Bluth Chorale, and asked us to be a part of it. As we got more exposure through performing with Bluth, Scott and I were asked more and more frequently to sing and play for firesides and perform special numbers for various LDS meetings throughout the Las Vegas valley.

Several people in the ward asked Scott to teach their children piano. He began giving piano lessons, and soon it became a lucrative part-time job in addition to his full-time job at the Stardust Hotel & Casino. Things were turning out wonderfully. Soon we were out of debt (except for the mortgage), fulfilled our pledge to the temple fund, and started building up a year's supply[1] of food and clothing as our church leaders directed.

With a new Bosch mixer, I was baking homemade bread with the best of the Saints. I even became determined to learn how to can food. I took my two oldest sons with me to go shopping for a canning pot. We bought five bushels of fruit so that I could "experience" canning. I felt I couldn't attain the full reaches of homemakerhood until I'd put up some fruit at least once. As we were driving, six-year-old Jeff noticed my keychain pepper spray canister on the dashboard. It was in the unlocked position from my previous night's errands. He picked it up.

"Look, Mom, it's unlocked. I'll lock it."

"You don't know how. Just leave it alone." I barely finished the sentence when *Psssst!* Jeff started screaming as it sprayed right into his face and the car quickly filled with stinging, burning fumes. Without thinking, my hand instinctively flew to my eyes and started rubbing, which only made things worse. I should have remembered from the Practical Motherhood Manual in the chapter entitled "Weapons A-Z," it says never to rub your eyes when tear gas residue is clinging to your eyeballs.

Seven-year-old Quinn started moaning and gasping in the back seat because it was too painful to breathe, and I began to cry. Squinting through my watering eyes to see where I was driving, I pulled up in front of a restaurant, managed to open the doors, and ran half-blinded past the hostess with two wailing kids in tow, mumbling incoherently something about stinging pepper. The heads of diners turned in succession like a field of wheat on a breezy day, as we flew past on our way to the restroom where we could rinse out our eyes. To our amazement, we discovered that the pepper spray had performed a pseudo-rhino-cilia-plasty on us (the non-surgical removal of nose hairs).

Red-eyed and crimson-faced we sheepishly scurried back past the curious diners, left the confused hostess staring after us, and resumed our journey in search of a canner. The boys must have thought I was out of my mind as I burst into uncontrollable laughter with tears streaming down my face.

"What's so funny?" they asked, still rubbing their sore eyes.

"I was just thinking about ten years from now when we look back on this and laugh."

I don't think canning is a major summer activity in Las Vegas, because after going to almost a dozen stores (especially exhausting after the pepper spray episode) all we found was a twenty-quart, poor quality, aluminum stock pot for less than ten dollars. At last we came across a rather expensive canner, got it home, and started the canning process. I went to put the lid on and it didn't fit. Upon close inspection we saw that the pot was warped. Well, I wasn't about to pay fifty dollars for a lousy pot. I knew where I could get a lousy pot for $7.99. We piled back into the car, surrounded by the lingering fumes of pepper now cemented to the upholstery, and returned the canner for a refund. We drove to the store which had the cheap one. By this time I decided that any pot would do to get us through this first miserable experience.

On the way out of the store we walked through the pet section to see the animals. There were some cute zebra finches on sale that were chirping wildly. The boys translated it as "Take us home." I gave the standard parental lecture on pets being a big responsibility and how they would need constant care and kind treatment. "We know," my sons reassured me. The birds were so pretty and the kids were excited about getting them, so I bought two. Jeff asked if he could carry the box.

"Yes, but be very careful with them," I admonished. As we were walking out to the car I heard frantic chirping behind me and turned to see Jeff "very carefully" swinging the box through the air lariat style. I'm surprised the centrifugal force allowed the poor creatures to make any sound while being plastered against the sides of the box.

"Holy mackerel," I exclaimed, wrenching the box of birds away from my gleeful son, and wondering if the kids were really ready to be pet owners. Eventually, we and our fine feathered friends made it safely home. Scott asked me if we were able to get our refund. I told him we not only got a refund, but found a much cheaper pot and two birds as well. After assuring him that I wasn't planning on pickling finches for food storage, we got down to the task of canning fruit. Maybe I would turn out to be Molly Mormon after all.

---

1. The Church recommends that members store a minimum one year supply of food, water, clothing, and fuel if possible, to prepare for unemployment, natural disaster, or an "End Times" scenario.

CHAPTER 7

The Three Nephites and Faith-promoting Rumors

I say "your civilization" because as soon as we start thinking for you, it really becomes our civilization; which is, of course, what this is all about.

—Agent Smith, The Matrix

He [Satan] wins a great victory when he can get members of the church to speak against their leaders and to "do their own thinking." . . . When our leaders speak, the thinking has been done.

— Improvement Era, June 1945, page 354, LDS Church

The last phase of completing the Las Vegas Temple was nearly finished. That summer I got a temporary part-time job with the landscaping company contracted to do the temple grounds. It was so exciting to me to be a part of the project. I felt like I was contributing to something eternal with every bush, shrub, and flower I planted. Such a wonderful variety of foliage was chosen; silver mullein, heavenly bamboo, petunias, Vinca rosea, and an array of palms, among other flora. I loved walking around the temple grounds when my shift was over. It felt so peaceful to be on a quiet part of town at the base of Frenchman Mountain, overlooking the valley.

For the first few years of our marriage we had to travel two hours north to St. George, Utah, to attend temple sessions. Normally, we rode with another couple or went with people from the ward on temple-trip days. The best thing about the temple (next to the spiritual enlightenment, of course) was the cafeteria. Ooh la la! The home-style foods and breads were amazing, and it was cheaper than eating at a restaurant.

On the long drive there and back we often got into deep discussions about End Time prophecies and what was going on in the Church as leaders prepared us for those events. It seemed we would always hear some new faith-promoting rumor that titillated our imaginations and inspired us to live the gospel more fully. One story was that So-and-so's brother and his wife went to the temple and on the way back saw three men hitchhiking. They usually avoided picking up hitchhikers, but this time they felt compelled to stop. On the drive, one of the men asked the couple if they had their year's supply of food. They answered affirmatively. The man told them it was a good thing because they would need it very soon. When the couple looked into the rearview mirror, they were shocked to find that all three men had disappeared.

Certainly the men were the Three Nephites, were they not? I loved hearing about Three Nephite sightings. It made me want to be more diligent in getting our year's supply of food. The Book of Mormon, 3 Nephi, chapter 28, contains the story of the Three Nephites. After Christ was resurrected, he appeared to the righteous Nephites and Lamanites here in the Americas choosing twelve disciples to teach and lead the people. When Jesus was about to ascend to heaven he asked the Twelve what they desired of him. Nine of them wanted to live to a normal age and when their earthly ministry was over to speedily go to heaven to be with the Lord.

The remaining three disciples were silent, too hesitant to voice their hearts' desire, which was to remain on the earth without tasting death until Christ should return at the end of the age. The Lord, knowing their thoughts, granted them their wish, commissioning them to minister incognito among the Gentiles and Jews, preaching the gospel and bringing people into the Church. My thoughts were that they were three Super Hero Bachelors who would be eligible for marriage in the Millennial Kingdom. If Scott didn't make it to the Celestial Kingdom and I did, I wondered if I could be given to Donny Osmond as a second wife or be a first wife to one of the Three Nephites. Of course, I wanted to be with Scott throughout all eternity, but like a good Cub Scouting/

Boy Scouting mom, I knew the value of being prepared for all possibilities. It never hurt to plan ahead.

Three Nephite sightings were not the only stories circulating among members. A few years later when senior apostle Gordon B. Hinckley became president of the Church, another faith-promoting rumor quickly spread. It always began with Sister and Brother So-and-So going to the Jordan Temple in southwest Salt Lake City on a Thursday evening. Normally this couple always took the stairs, but because of a sprained ankle or arthritis flare-up they took the elevator. Much to their surprise and delight, President Hinckley was in the elevator. Before the door opened on the next floor, he turned to them and asked if they had their food storage, to which they replied no but were working on getting it. Nodding gravely, President Hinckley admonished them to hurry because time was short.

I decided that next time I was in Utah I would attend a session in the Jordan Temple on the chance I could meet the prophet in the elevator. Of course I'd have to break a leg or something first, as temple elevators were generally restricted to the aged, decrepit, or VIPs (or for aged, decrepit VIPs). Maybe the prophet or some of the apostles would attend the Las Vegas Temple someday, and I would have the privilege of going through an endowment session with them or eating in the cafeteria at the same time. I could just picture standing in the line at lunch and while reaching for a whole wheat roll Bruce R. McConkie steps next to me and asks, "Sister, do you have your year's supply of food?" After picking myself up off the floor I say, "Not yet, but we're close."

"Sister, you really must hurry."

"Is that because the seven-year tribulation is about to start and we'll have to walk to Jackson County, Missouri?"

"No, it's because I have a meeting with the temple president in five minutes and you're holding up the line."

Of the Faith Promoting Rumors that abounded, the Three Nephites and President Hinckley in the temple elevator were clearly my two favorites. I was skeptical about most of the variations, but believed they were all spun off of true accounts.

A public open house for the Las Vegas Temple was scheduled for November 16 through December 9, 1989. We took all of our children including 18-month-old Curran, who, I hoped, would keep the memory of it somewhere in the recesses of his mind and someday have a vision of how beautiful and peaceful the temple was. Despite our attempts at making this event a spiritual experience, seven-year-old Jeff complained the whole time, running ahead of us so he could periodically sit on the floor and rest until we caught up.

The day finally came for the Las Vegas Temple to be dedicated. The dedication took place during 11 sessions from December 16th to the 18th, to accommodate all the recommend-holders in the valley. Our assigned session was Sunday morning. Only those with recommends could attend. Children over age eight could go after having a bishop's interview to determine worthiness. Eight-year-old Quinn was sick with a headache and stomach pains the night before, feeling only a little better that morning.

After parking a few blocks from the temple and walking the rest of the way, we were seated in a little overflow room close to the men's locker area, with only a handful of people with us. It was a nice service. Quinn slept almost the whole time, snoring lightly between jabs from my elbow. I woke him up for the "Hosanna Shout," which sounded more like a Hosanna Mumble from everyone present. We all sang the hymn *The Spirit of God Like a Fire is Burning*, which made me choke up. It was the same song we sang at my baptism years before. We were well on our way to being an eternal family. My heart was bursting with joy over having a temple so close to home and being a constant reminder to our kids of greater things to come.

The week after the April 1990 General Conference, a new movie was released for the temple, replacing older versions. I left the temple exhilarated after seeing it for the first time. It was so realistic and made me even more aware of Satan's plan to destroy mankind. We are his enemies because we turned down his proposed plan of salvation in the preexistence.

According to Mormon doctrine, everyone lived on a world near a star named Kolob in a galaxy far, far away. We were in spirit form without physical bodies; children of a heavenly Father and Mother(s), raised and nurtured in the "courts on high." Mormonism teaches that;

> "Every person who was ever born on earth was our spirit brother or sister in heaven. The first spirit born to our heavenly parents was Jesus Christ (see D&C 93:21), so he is literally our elder brother (see *Discourses of Brigham Young*, p. 26). Because we are the spiritual children of our heavenly parents, we have inherited the potential to develop their divine qualities. If we choose to do so, we can become perfect, just as they are."[1]

When we all became fully grown spirit beings it was time for the next phase of our eternal progression; the Second Estate, which essentially meant birth into mortal bodies on an earth prepared just for that purpose. It was to be a place where we could experience opposition in all things and be given "Free Agency" to choose righteousness or wickedness.

Our Second Estate was to be a proving ground to test whether human souls would "do all things whatsoever the Lord their God shall command them" (Abraham 3:25, Pearl of Great Price). If we kept our Second Estate, faithfully obeying all the laws and ordinances of the gospel (which includes baptism into the Mormon Church, receiving temple endowments, and living a life of worthiness), we would be able to attain the Celestial Kingdom, which is the highest degree of glory in the next life. Making it to the highest level within the Celestial Kingdom would allow us to progress to become gods of our own worlds at some point and have spirit children of our own who would go through the same process, and so on throughout eternity.

Prior to being born on this earth a grand council was convened, and all the spirit beings gathered to listen to Heavenly Father's plan for our salvation. This plan required us to come to earth to be tried and tested and be given the opportunity to advance to godhood. Jesus stepped forward and volunteered to become the savior, offering his life as atonement for the sins we would commit. He agreed with Heavenly Father that we needed the freedom to choose for ourselves whether or not to follow him. Only in this way could it be determined if we were worthy to be exalted in the afterlife.

Then Lucifer came forward volunteering to redeem mankind by forcing everyone to be obedient, thus losing no one in the process; the only caveat being that he would get all the glory. After hearing both proposals Heavenly Father declared, "I will send the first." Rebuffed and chagrined, Lucifer flew into a rage and rebelled against the authority of heaven, supported by a third of Heavenly Father's children. A war in heaven ensued. Lucifer became Satan. The fallen spirit beings fought against Jesus and the rest of the heavenly hosts until they were cast out of God's presence. These fallen beings became the bodiless demons that tempt and seduce mankind.

The movie shown in the temple endowment session was a reenactment of events purported to have happened in the preexistence and the Garden of Eden (or at least symbolic of it), with pre-incarnate appearances of Jesus, Peter, James, and John (played by LDS actors, of course). The scenes depict the priesthood holders following orders and giving instructions to Adam and Eve, then reporting back to "Elohim" (the personal name of God the Father according to Mormon teachings).

The most chilling scene in the film is when the character of Satan, played by LDS music professor and performer Michael Ballam, looks directly into the camera and warns;

> "I have a word to say concerning these people. If they do not walk up to every covenant they make at these altars in this temple this day, they will be in my power!"

One thing I had absolutely *no* interest in was being in Satan's power! I would need to commit myself to even deeper personal prayer and study. The only way we could be assured of keeping ourselves from the Devil's grasp was to obey the prophet and follow the counsel of our leaders. President Ezra Taft Benson, in an address given at Brigham Young University, stated;

> It will be your responsibility not only to help to carry the kingdom to a triumph but to save your own soul and strive to save those of your family and to honor the principles of the inspired Constitution of the United States.[2]

After seeing the new temple film for the first time, I called my sister-in-law Kay, with whom I was close, to talk about spiritual matters and how to improve our walk with the Lord. At the end of our hour-long conversation, I agreed to read from the Book of Mormon and the U.S. Constitution 30 minutes a day.

---

1. Gospel Principles, *Our Heavenly Family* (The Church of Jesus Christ of Latter-day Saints: Salt Lake City, UT, 1997), 11.
2. Ezra Taft Benson, Fourteen Fundamentals in Following the Prophet. *Liahona*, June Issue, 1981. Can also be found on LDS.org and other places on the web.

CHAPTER 8

Preparing for the Last Days

It is obvious that you are an intelligent man, Mr. Anderson, and that you are interested in the future.

—Agent Smith, The Matrix

The Constitution was almost like Scripture; divinely inspired and playing a significant role in Mormon "End-time" prophecy. LDS President George Albert Smith stated, "I am saying to you that to me the Constitution of the United States of America is just as much from my Heavenly Father as the Ten Commandments."[1]

We were taught that one day the Constitution would "hang by a thread," and the Elders of the Church would step forward and rescue it. I loved reading about the great Constitution of the United States of America and how the Founding Fathers were valiant spirits in the preexistent life, reserved to come down to the earth at the proper time to establish a free nation in which the gospel—revealed to Joseph Smith, Jr.—could flourish. I studied to find all the teachings and doctrines I could on the subject of Mormonism and the Last Days and our role as members of the Church in ushering in the Second Coming of Jesus Christ. Following are some of the teachings that inspired, encouraged, and concerned me, and a few that even frightened me:

President Ezra Taft Benson (13th president of the Church) warned,

We are fast approaching that moment prophesied by Joseph

Smith when he said: "Even the nation will be on the very verge of crumbling to pieces and tumbling to the ground, and when the Constitution is upon the brink of ruin, this people will be the staff upon which the nation will lean, and they shall bear the Constitution away from the very verge of destruction."

I have faith that the Constitution will be saved as prophesied by Joseph Smith. But it will not be saved from Washington. It will be saved by the citizens of this nation who love and cherish freedom. It will be saved by enlightened members of this Church—men and women who will subscribe to and abide the principles of the Constitution.[2]

President David O. McKay (ninth president of the Church) wrote,

Next to being one in worshiping God, there is nothing in this world upon which this church should be more united than in upholding and defending the Constitution of the United States![3]

President John Taylor (third president of the Church) said,

And now, you may write it down, any of you, and I will prophesy it in the name of God. And then will be fulfilled that prediction to be found in one of the revelations given through the prophet Joseph Smith. Those who will not take up their sword to fight against their neighbor must needs flee to Zion for safety. And they will come, saying, we do not know anything of the principles of your religion, but we perceive that you are an honest community; you administer justice and righteousness, and we want to live with you and receive the protection of your laws, but as for your religion we will talk about that some other time. Will we protect such people? Yes, all honorable men. When the people have torn to shreds the Constitution of the United States the Elders of Israel will be found holding it up to the nations of the earth and proclaiming liberty and equal rights to all men, and extending the hand of fellowship to the oppressed of all nations.[4]

Joseph Smith warned;

And now I am prepared to say by the authority of Jesus Christ, that not many years shall pass away before the United States shall present such a scene of bloodshed as has not a parallel in the history of our nation; pestilence, hail, famine, and earthquake will sweep the wicked of this generation off the face of the land, to open and prepare the way for the return of the lost tribes of Israel from the north country.[5]

LDS Apostle Orson Pratt spoke at a conference saying,

What then will be the condition of that people [Americans], when this great and terrible war shall come? It will be very different from the war between the North and the South. Do you wish me to describe it? I will do so. It will be a war of neighborhood against neighborhood, city against city, town against town, county against county, state against state, and they will go forth destroying and being destroyed and manufacturing will in a great measure, cease, for a time, among the American nation. Why? Because in these terrible wars, they will not be privileged to manufacture; there will be too much bloodshed—too much mobocracy—too much going forth in bands and destroying and pillaging the land to suffer people to pursue any local vocation with any degree of safety. What will become of millions of the farmers upon that land? They will leave their farms and they will remain uncultivated, and they will flee before the ravaging armies from place to place; and thus they will go forth burning and pillaging the whole country...Now these are predictions you may record. You may let them sink down into your hearts. And if the Lord your God shall permit you to live, you will see my words fulfilled to the very letter. They are not my words, but the words of inspiration—the words of the everlasting God, who has sent forth his servants with this message to warn the nations of the earth.[6]

Probably the most alarming prophecy I read was of a vision President John Taylor had of the destruction of the United States. It's rather lengthy and there seems to be a couple slightly different versions, but excerpts are included here because it's vital to understanding my beliefs as a Mormon and part of what motivated me to be as faithful a member of the Church as possible. Wilford Woodruff recorded Taylor's vision in his journal;

> I went to bed as usual at about 7:30PM. I had been reading a revelation in the French language. My mind was calm, more so than usual if possible, so I composed myself for sleep, but could not. I felt a strange feeling come over me and apparently became partially unconscious. Still I was not asleep, nor exactly awake, with dreary feeling. The first thing that I recognized was that I was in the tabernacle of Ogden, Utah. I was sitting in the back part of the building for fear they would call on me to preach, which however they did, for after singing the second time they called me to the stand.
>
> I arose to speak and said that I didn't know that I had anything especially to say, except to bear my testimony of the Latter-day work, when all at once it seemed as if I was lifted out of myself and I said, "Yes, I have something to say and that is this: Some of my brethren have been asking, "What is becoming of us? What is the wind blowing?" I will answer you right here what is coming very shortly."
>
> I was then in a dream immediately in the city of Salt Lake walking through the streets. In parts of the city and upon the door of every house, I saw a badge of mourning and I could not find a house but what was in mourning. I passed my own home and saw the same sign there. I asked the question, "Is that me who is dead?"
>
> Something gave the answer, "No. You will get through it all."
>
> It seemed strange to me that I saw no person on the streets in my wandering around the city. They seemed to be in their houses with their sick and dead. I saw no funeral processions or anything of this kind, but the city was very still and quiet as if the people were praying. It seemed as though the people had control over the disease, whatever it was, I do not know, that was not shown to me.
>
> I then looked in all directions over the territory; east, west, north and south, and found the same mourning in every place throughout the land.
>
> The next I knew I was this side of Omaha. It seemed I was above the earth looking down upon it as I passed along on my way east. I saw the roads full of people, principally women, with just what they could carry in bundles on their backs, traveling to

the mountains on foot. And I wondered how they would get there with nothing but a small pack on their backs. It was remarkable to me that there were so few men among them. It did not seem as though trains were running; the rails looked rusty and the roads abandoned. Indeed, I have no conception of how I traveled myself as I looked down upon the people.

I continued east through Omaha and Council Bluffs, which were full of disease, and women were everywhere. The streets of Missouri and Illinois were in turmoil and strife. Men were killing one another, and women joined in the fighting. Family against family was cutting each other to pieces in the most horrible manner imaginable.

Next I saw Washington, D.C., and found the city a desolation. The White House was empty and the Halls of Congress likewise. Everything was in ruin and the people seemed to have fled from the city and left it to take care of itself.

I was next in the city of Baltimore, in the square where the monument of 1812 stands in front of the St. Charles and other hotels. The dead were everywhere. I saw their bodies piled up, filling the square. I saw women cut the throats of their own children for the sake of their blood. I saw them suck it from their veins to quench their own thirst and then lie down in the streets and die.

The waters of the city and the Chesapeake Bay were so stagnant, and such a stench arose from them on account of the putrefaction of the dead carcasses in them, that the very smell carried death with it.

Singularly again, I saw no men, except they were dead or dying in the streets. There were but very few women, and they were crazy and mad, or in a dying condition. Everywhere I went I saw the same all over the city. It was horrible beyond conception to behold.

I thought this was the end; but not so. Seemingly in an instant I was in Philadelphia where everything was still. No living soul was to be seen to greet me. It seemed as though the whole city was without inhabitants. In Arch and Chestnut streets, in fact, everywhere I looked the putrefaction of the dead bodies created such a stench that it was impossible for any creature to remain alive.

I next found myself on Broadway in New York. There it seemed as if the people had done all they could to overcome the disease. But in wandering down Broadway, I saw the bodies of beautiful women lying, some dead, and others in a dying condition, on the sidewalks. I saw men crawl out of the basements and violate the persons of some that were alive, then kill them and rob their dead bodies of the valuables they had on them. Then, before they could return to their basements, they themselves rolled over a time or two in agony and died.

On some of the streets I saw mothers kill their own offspring and eat their flesh, and then in a few minutes die themselves. And wherever I looked, I saw the same sights,--horror and desolation, rapine and death. No horses, nor carriages, nor omnibuses, nor streetcars,--nothing but death and destruction everywhere.

I then went to Central Park, and looking back, I saw a fire start, and just at that moment a mighty east wind sprang up and carried the flames west over the great city. And it burned until there was not a single building left standing whole; even down to the water's edge.--Wharves and shipping--all seemed to be burned and swallowed up in common destruction. Nothing was left but desolation where a great city stood a short time before. Stench from the bodies that were burned was so great that it was carried a great distance across the Hudson River, and it spread disease and death wherever the fumes penetrated.

I cannot paint in words the horrors that seemed to encompass me about, it was beyond description or thought for me to conceive.

I suppose this was the end, but I was given to understand that the same horrors that were here enacted were all over the world, east, west, north, and south--That few were left alive--still there were some.

Immediately after, I seemed to be standing on the left bank of the Missouri River, opposite the city of Independence;--but I saw no city. I saw the whole states of Illinois and Missouri and part of Iowa, a complete wilderness of desert with no living human being there.

I then saw a short distance from the river, twelve men draped in the robes of the Temple, standing in a square, or nearly so. I understood it to represent the twelve gates of the New Jerusalem. And they with uplifted hands, were consecrating the ground and laying the cornerstone of the Temple.

And while they were thus employed, I saw myriads of angels hovering over them and around them. And I heard the angels singing the most heavenly music. The words were: "Now is established the Kingdom of God and His Christ, and He shall reign forever and ever! And the Kingdom shall never be thrown down, for the Saints have overcome!"

I saw people coming from the river and from distant places to help build the Temple and the City. It seemed as though there were hosts of angels helping to bring material for the construction of that building. Some were in Temple robes, and the pillar-like cloud continued to hover over the spot…I rolled over on my bed and the clock struck twelve. The vision had occurred between 9:30 P.M. and midnight.[7]

These prophecies by LDS leaders intrigued and disturbed me. I knew that we—as Mormons and a nation—were headed for trouble and needed to be prepared. I also knew that the Latter-day Saints would save the day and I would get to be a part of it. I wanted to help "build the kingdom" in some way or another. The big question was how.

---

1. *Conference Report*, April 1948, p. 182
2. Ezra Taft Benson. "The Constitution: A Heavenly Banner," *BYU Speeches*, 1986. Retrieved from http://speeches.byu.edu/?act=viewitem&id=87. Also available in booklet form.
3. The Instructor. (1957). 91:34
4. Journal of Discourses, Vol. 21, p.8
5. Joseph Smith, *Documented History of the Church, Vol. 1*, January 4, 1833. 315-316
6. *Journal of Discourses, Vol. 20*, Sunday, March 9, 1879. 150-151
7. Wilford Woodruff Journal, June 15, 1878. *"A Vision, Salt Lake City, Night of December 16, 1877."* This account of Taylor's vision has been circulated over the years, ending up in several print publications and on the web.

CHAPTER 9

Ain't Misbehavin'

Zion is the place, man. You'll see it one day. Last human city. All we got left.
—Tank, The Matrix

I was always drawn to singing. From the time I was a young child I loved music, singing, and writing. I crafted mock microphones out of construction paper, the cardboard tubes from toilet paper rolls, and in a pinch, a pen or hairbrush handle. I put my favorite record albums on my portable record player, cranked up the volume, and sang as if I were on stage in front of thousands of people. When I didn't want to just imagine it, I would call my family in and have them sit on the couch and watch me. Of course, they would cheer and applaud wildly. I felt like I could change the world somehow with my singing, and that desire got stronger as the years went by.

When Scott and I first started doing professional gigs, apparently we weren't as good as we thought. Okay, I'll admit it; I was the one with illusions of grandeur. Scott was a tad more realistic about our limitations. My voice was often flat (or so I was told), and Scott didn't know many riffs on the piano. Our repertoire consisted of about 25 tunes; a mix of Big Band, standards, show tunes, some classical, and a couple songs we had written. You can only sing 25 songs night after night off-key before people don't want to hear any more (and I don't mean they would rather be deaf than listen to us play).

We literally had a captive audience in Salt Lake City's Hotel Newhouse dining room. You see, the majority of diners were senior citizens who lived in the hotel. There was nowhere else for them to go for dinner; at least nowhere close by. We played there three nights a week for $15 a night, which we split. I clearly remember, after months of performing we learned a new song from the 1930's, "When I Take My Sugar to Tea." We got a standing ovation. We thought the seniors loved that song and started playing it a couple times a night. The enthusiasm of our audience quickly dissipated after a few days. Much to our chagrin, we realized they had applauded because we finally did something new, not because they liked the song.

One night we were in the middle of a set, and I asked the audience if they had any requests. A big, burly man stood up and crossed the room. Taking out his wallet, he slapped a five dollar bill on top of the piano and with a loud Texas accent drawled, "Yeah, I've got a request. Don't sing 'til I'm done eating." Then he turned around and went back to his table. Scott and I looked at each other, shrugged, took the five dollars and went on break with big grins on our faces. That was the biggest tip we had ever gotten.

Happily, over time, through dedicated practice and training, Scott and I became respected musicians. Deep inside I knew I had a special mission on earth and believed Heavenly Father would use my singing to bring people into the Church. It wasn't long before we were asked on a regular basis to sing special numbers for Sacrament Meeting in our own and other wards, Stake Conferences, Relief Society functions, firesides, and other Church-sponsored events. Scott always had a knack for embellishing a simple hymn or Children's Primary song and turning it into a grandiose, emotionally-moving piece. One of our signature medleys was a combination of *America the Beautiful* and the LDS hymn *Because I Have Been Given Much*. Ward members always came up to us afterward with tears in their eyes, telling us how touched they were. It really encouraged me.

I met a woman in our stake, Pat Pymm, who was taking singing lessons from a professional singer who studied under the renowned Seth Riggs of Hollywood. Pat offered to teach me what she was learning. We became close friends, and I ended up taking weekly lessons from her and performing in recitals for the following 17 years. She was an amazing woman who I have a great deal of love and respect for to this very day.

One day after my lesson was over, Pat said, "Tracy, you've got to hear the most awesome song I've ever heard. I swear it will make you cry." She put in a cassette tape and played a song called "Unshakeable Kingdom" by Christian recording artist Sandi Patty. We sat there completely mesmerized by the words and Sandi's phenomenal voice. Before the song was halfway over we both had tears streaming down our faces. All I could say when the last note faded was "Wow!" I asked Pat where she got the tape. She told me she got it at a Christian bookstore after hearing the song on the radio. Up until then I didn't even know there was such a thing as Christian bookstores, or radio stations playing Christian music for that matter. On the way home from Pat's house I found the store and bought my first Christian music tape; Sandi Patty's album "Morning Like This."

Sandi's music had a serious impact on my life. I played her tape every day when I was in the kitchen cooking or doing dishes, which seemed to be where I spent most of my time with a family of seven to feed. I sang along at the top of my voice, frequently choking up during some of the songs. My heart soared listening to Sandi, especially when she hit those high notes with the background music reaching its climax. How I longed to sing like Sandi!

Pat and I began working on the songs from Sandi's tapes at our weekly lessons. It really puzzled us how Christians could come up with such powerful music and inspiring lyrics when they didn't even have the true gospel. They wrote and sang as if they knew the Lord on a personal basis. We often lamented that LDS music wasn't as powerful. The songs were sweet and pretty to us, but not very compelling.

From that point on, whenever I was asked to sing a special number at church I always sang a Sandi Patty song. Sometimes we had to tone down the ending a bit to make it more suitable for Sacrament Meeting. Other times I had to change some of the lyrics to bring it in line with Mormon doctrine. In all cases, however, ward members made sure to express how moved they were by the music and how they had never heard anything like it. They asked where the songs came from and I would answer that it was by a Christian singer named Sandi Patty. Naturally, no one had heard of her before. As Mormons, we generally didn't listen to popular Christian music.

The ward music chairman always asked me in advance what I would be singing. I would tell her the name of the song, which she would always be unfamiliar with. Finally she told me in exasperation, "Sister Crookston, the *Church Handbook of Instructions* advises using songs from the Church hymn book or Primary songbook and to avoid popular styles of music. I have to make sure the music is appropriate for Sacrament Meeting."

One time I replied, "The song *is* appropriate, I promise. Just tell the Bishop I didn't give you the name of the song yet, this way you won't be responsible if there's a problem." With a heavy sigh she walked away, knowing there was no arguing with me when it came to picking songs. Suffice it to say, I never had a complaint from our leaders. Every Bishop we ever had always said something encouraging about our special numbers. The best thing that happened was when I was called to be the new ward music chairman, because then I sang whatever I wanted to without worrying about getting anyone's approval first.

During one of my singing lessons, Pat gave me the most exciting news. She had been asked to sing in a Sunday service at a Christian church. We believed the Lord was giving her the opportunity to do some missionary work bringing the LDS gospel to Christians. Over the next several months Pat was asked to sing at one predominantly black church after another in North Las Vegas. We could only attribute these opportunities to the Lord.

Nevertheless, I felt a little bummed out over this turn of events. Pat always wanted her special mission to be within the Church, making a difference in the lives of members. I always wanted my mission to be outside the Church, touching the hearts of non-members and bringing them into the fold of Mormonism. However, my opportunities to sing and speak within the Church were increasing, while Pat kept getting more invitations outside the Church. It was all backwards. I supposed that was the way things worked in our eternal progression; doing what Heavenly Father wanted us to do, rather than following our own desires. I guess I could live with that. I just wanted with all my heart to do something important.

Scott and I were invited to be a part of the Bluth (rhymes with tooth) Chorale, led by the talented, witty, musical genius, Bruce Green. The Chorale was an all LDS choir composed of some of the best vocalists in the valley. While most of the songs we performed were by LDS composers, a fair portion of them were Christian hymn arrangements, ones not found in our LDS hymn book. Bluth normally put on two major concerts a year; one at Christmas and one around Easter, but this year Bruce wanted to let loose and do a fun fall jazz concert. Scott was given a piano solo; a flamboyant, entertaining piece which he arranged, entitled *Ludwig Had a Boogie Lamb*. It was a conglomeration of Beethoven, Mary Had a Little Lamb, and the Bumble Boogie, with bits of other songs peppered throughout the piece. I got to sing an amazing rendition of the 1929 Fat's Waller song, "Ain't Misbehavin."

I loved being a part of Bluth! Every time I sang it felt like a conduit opened up between me and heaven, especially when I sang Christian songs. Somehow I felt closer to Jesus when singing. I looked on him as my older brother—certainly more advanced in his progression than I was—and wondered if thousands of years in the future one of my own spirit sons would have to be a savior on one of the world's my husband would organize. I hoped not, even though some of my relatives speculated otherwise. They said there would always have to be a savior appointed for each new "round of creation."

I didn't want to think about that. I didn't want to think about that any more than I wanted to think about polygamy in the next life. I put those concerns on a back burner and decided to just focus on my mission and what I was supposed to do in *this* life. Singing, speaking, teaching; these are the things I dreamed of doing. I could see myself being a speaker at BYU Education Week,[1] or even teaching seminary. I was ready for a change of direction in my life. It was soon to come.

---

1. Every year, the third week of August is reserved at Brigham Young University for a CES (Church Educational System) event. Classes are held from about 8:25 a.m. to 9:25 p.m. on a variety of church-related topics; homemaking, food storage, parenting, church history, doctrinal themes, and even select secular classes like ballroom dance, gardening, or interior design.

CHAPTER 10

Motherhood and Mayhem

As children we do not separate the possible from the impossible; which is why the younger a mind is, the easier it is to free, while a mind like yours can be very difficult.

—Morpheus, The Matrix

The Bishopric called, asking if they could come over. We had just moved again into a bigger house to accommodate our growing family, which now numbered eight; Scott, me, five boys, and one girl. Now the Bishopric was here to welcome us into the Curtis Park Ward in the Meadows Stake. We sat and visited for a while as they asked us about our family and what positions we held in the Church so far.

"I'll accept whatever calling I'm given," I said, "but I do have one request, if that's all right. I've taught Primary for the last seven years. If it doesn't really matter to the Lord, it would really be nice to not be in the Primary anymore. I *live with* the Primary! We home school our six children and I'm with them 24 hours a day. Then I come to church and teach everyone else's children. I'd like some adult companionship. But only if that's okay with the Lord."

"Well Sister Crookston," the Bishop said, "we appreciate your honesty and your willingness to serve. We'll pray about this and see what the Lord has for you."

The Lord had a lot in store for me in that ward over the subsequent seven years we lived there. First, I was called to be the assistant ward librarian, where

I served for a year. I learned how to conduct after being called to lead music in Relief Society, became Ward Music Chairman, and prepared the weekly bulletin for Sacrament Meeting.

Being in the library where I handed materials to Primary and Sunday school teachers was more relaxing than teaching CTR (Choose The Right) or Valiant classes (for children ages 4 through 11). Over the years, leadership always seemed to have me teach whatever class the most wild of my sons was in. Some of my boys were…well…there's no delicate way to put it; they were brats. I hate to digress (well, not really), but I have to pause for a station break to expound on what I was dealing with as a Mormon mother of five, six, seven, and eventually ten children. Hopefully, this will stir some compassion for mothers with small children, but especially if you are LDS, a bit more empathy for big families in your ward that kind of irritate you during Sacrament Meeting because of their unruly behavior. If you're not LDS, but know some families that are, perhaps you'll have a better understanding of what typically occurs.

In traditional Mormon families, mom stays at home and dad goes to work, sometimes working a second job to support the family. Mom is the primary caregiver, being around children almost all the time; their own, neighborhood children, children of other ward members who are being babysat, and children that seem to appear out of nowhere.

Additionally, mom and dad have multiple callings in the Church, including home and visiting teaching positions. That would be challenging in and of itself, but now throw into the mix the pressure (self-imposed, as well as real or perceived expectations within Mormonism) to be perfect, worthy, righteous, and a good example to others. How your children "turn out" becomes a reflection of your personal righteousness and worth. When leaders, such as President Joseph F. Smith, say things like this, it can be quite overwhelming;

> Not one child in a hundred would go astray, if the home environment, example and training, were in harmony with the truth of the gospel of Christ, as revealed and taught to the Latter-day Saint. Fathers and mothers, you are largely to blame for the infidelity and indifference of your children. You can remedy the evil by earnest worship, example, training, and discipline in the home.[1]

Here are some examples, taken from my journals, of the challenges I had as the main disciplinarian of my children. It's not funny when you're going through experiences like these, but years later you look back and laugh.

Sunday (Circa 1987)

We got to church a few minutes early for a change. We sat in an empty pew and got settled. Sister Whittaker came and sat in front of us. She's the real nervous type and I was worried our family would disturb her during the meeting. No sooner had I told the kids they would need to sit still and be especially reverent, when Tristan went tumbling along the bench doing forward rolls at breakneck speed.

"Tristan," I quickly warned, "Stop, before you hit..." It was too late. His skinny little legs, clad with oversized cowboy boots, came up and whacked Sister Whittaker right on the side of her head, which kind of snapped to the side. I was completely mortified!

"Oh my! Sister Whittaker! Are you okay? I am so sorry!" She just sat there a bit stunned, staring with wide eyes like a deer caught in headlights. "Sister Whittaker?" I wondered if she had a concussion. I scooped up the kids, diaper bag, activity books, Cheerios, and all other paraphernalia and slinked to the back of the chapel. I prayed she came to her senses before the meeting started. Maybe by the time she regained consciousness she wouldn't know who or what hit her.

May 18, 1988

I met Scott at President and Sister Waite's house so we could have our temple recommend interviews. After Scott's was finished, Sister Waite told him he could leave and she would watch the kids while I had my interview. It was a disaster! Jeff and Tristan ran around their house, darting up and down the hallway, not obeying Sister Waite at all. Summer kept coming in and out of President Waite's office. The interview seemed to drag on forever while I sat worrying what in the world was going on in the rest of the house. Finally it was time to leave. Jeff and Tristan ran outside and jumped in the van, locked the doors, and Tristan laid on the horn just to listen to it reverberate throughout the neighborhood. My banging on the window only made them laugh and honk all the more. One of the interview questions was if I abused my children in any way. Of course the answer was no, but I sure felt like giving my recommend back to President Waite so I could dole out some heavy discipline on the boys.

September 24, 1988

It's getting harder to find babysitters. The last time we needed one, we finally found a teenage boy in the ward willing to come over. It was a catastrophe. When we got home all the kids and the sitter were out in the front yard and all the windows and doors were wide open. Apparently, Joseph (the babysitter) found my self-defense pepper spray and emptied it in the house. Plus, the kids' bedroom window had a big gaping hole in it. Joseph and the kids were throwing large waffle blocks at each other and one of them went hurtling through the window pane. I can't believe we actually paid him. We should have sent him a bill.

So, this time we recruited Aunt Al to come watch the kids for a few hours. We came home to a cacophony of screaming children. Tristan was crying from under his bedroom door. Poor Aunt Al was struggling to drag Jeff down the hall, yelling at him to get into his room and behave. Quinn was jumping from couch to couch. Summer was singing at the top of her voice. Aunt Al told us she was never going to babysit again. She said the kids were rotten all evening, tormenting each other and her. I don't know why they have been so "monsterish" lately.

January 8, 1989

Today the kids advanced to the next level in Primary. Tristan did *not* want to go to his new Star-A class. He said, "I hate my new teacher! I'll *never* like her. I'll *always* hate her! I only like Sister Hartzell" (the Sunbeam teacher). After class, when we were in the foyer, Tristan said he would only go to Star-A next week if he could kiss Sister Hartzell on the knees. Before we could stop him he ran up to her, flipped up her skirt, and kissed both her kneecaps! Then he demanded that she let him kiss her bare eyeballs. She obviously didn't want him kissing her eyes, especially after her embarrassing kneecap exposure (let's just say the flipping of the skirt revealed a little more than her knees), but she finally consented to letting him kiss her eyelids. Sometimes that boy is strange.

December 1989

One night this month Scott was working and my parents and Aunt Al went out on the town, leaving me at home to take care of Grammy (who has Alzheimer's) and the kids. Tristan and Summer put their money together a few weeks ago to buy a pair of toy handcuffs, which soon broke, leaving only the plastic key. So Summer comes into the kitchen crying really hard, pointing to her nose. There was the handcuff key protruding from one of her nostrils. I tried to gently remove it, but it was stuck fast. No matter which direction I tugged, the key would not come out. So, I started crying, which made Summer wail all the louder. I didn't know what else to do, so I called 911 and explained the situation. Guess I should have called a locksmith instead. A few minutes later Summer started laughing through her tears, holding the key in her hand. I asked her how she got it out. "I don't know Mommy. I just turned the key and my nose opened." I called the paramedics and told them they didn't need to come.

That's just a flavor of our home life while Scott worked 60-plus hours a week. Things weren't *always* that awful. On the one hand, we had probably the rowdiest kids in the ward for a long time, but we also had the smartest, wittiest, and most talented (in my humble opinion). Ward leaders and teachers were always amazed at how much our kids knew about the gospel. They had all 13 Articles of Faith and the Ten Commandments memorized, as well as key Book of Mormon verses. They knew about doctrines the average church member was unfamiliar with, sometimes adding insights to their Sunday school and Aaronic priesthood teacher's lessons. This knowledge came from our daily "family goals," which included family Scripture reading, prayer, singing a song, reading a General Conference talk, and following up with discussion. Each of the kids also had a daily piano lesson from their dad.

After having an idea of what our home life was like, it's easy to see how I could want something different than a calling in the Primary. I knew how important the Primary was, but I needed some encouragement and interaction with the ladies in the ward. My calling to serve as assistant librarian was a nice change, but it was a rather lonely job.

I told Scott about my desire to be in Relief Society. He said, "Here is what you need to do. Go talk to the Relief Society teachers and offer to substitute for them if they go out of town or get sick. It's usually hard to find people willing to sub, so that's a sure way to get your foot in the door."

That's exactly what I did. I offered to teach people's lessons if they had to miss a Sunday. One teacher left every summer to be with her family out of state, so I had three months to teach on her designated Sunday. I loved teaching and always tried to make the lessons interesting and engaging. It was so important to me to make a difference in the lives of the sisters. I received a lot of positive feedback. It was only a couple months after Sister Merritt returned that she was released from her position, and I was called to be the new "Spiritual Living" teacher in Relief Society.

Life was taking an exciting turn in terms of spiritual growth and motherhood. My older children were becoming teenagers. I wondered what lay in store for me.

---

1. Improvement Era, Vol. 7, Dec., 1904, 135. Also; Joseph F. Smith, Gospel Doctrine, 5th ed., Salt Lake City: Deseret Book Co., 1939, 302.

CHAPTER 11

High Speed Chase

...I don't like the idea that I'm not in control of my life.

—Neo, The Matrix

The stringy-haired blonde stuck her head out the window and yelled a line of obscenities that would have made even a liberal politician blush. I looked at the old, beat-up hillbilly pickup truck in the lane next to us. You'd have thought we put a dent in their Mercedes Benz. A man and two females stared at us, scowls on their faces. Quinn, typical 13-year-old, snickered from the back seat where he'd used a straw like a pea-shooter to blow a small chunk of ice out the window. The projectile bounced off the hillbilly's truck, melting onto the hot blacktop. The traffic signal turned green and the truck peeled out abruptly with one of the women's hand still giving me a one-fingered salute.

This was Utah for crying out loud; the land of milk and honey, the land of courteous citizens with friendly smiles and hardy handshakes. The barbarians in the pickup were an anomaly.

"You should have your mouth washed out with soap!" I yelled in return, indignant over the verbal assault and slightly miffed at my son's recklessness. Having gotten that off my chest, and scolding Quinn for blowing ice at strangers, I turned into the shopping center parking lot. Mr. Redneck and his wife and girl-friend apparently saw us turning into the same shopping center they had turned into, because here they came barreling over speed bumps heading straight for our car. I tried to turn the car around, but it was too late for such a maneuver. In seconds the driver would be pulled up alongside of my window.

"Okay. This is it," I thought in a panic. "Country Boy is going to pull his rifle off the gun rack and blow my head off over an ice cube." Have you ever heard someone exclaim that their life passed before their eyes in only a moment? For the first time I knew exactly what that meant. I braced myself for a confrontation as the man came to a screeching halt next to us, with mere fractions of an inch between our vehicles. His teeth were yellow, and I could count the pockmarks on his face. The faint scent of chewing tobacco permeated his breath, which came in short bursts of volatile anger. Suddenly, the will to survive welled up inside of me as I declared, "Today is *not* a good day for dying," and stepped on the gas pedal.

I raced away across the parking lot with the Dukes of Hazzard in hot pursuit, flying over speed bumps, staying far from pedestrians, looking for escape. My eyes were glued to the rearview mirror; I could see the truck gaining speed, the gap between us closing. Noticing a break between buildings, I made a sharp turn and found myself on a back street behind the shopping center. I sped toward the main road. In the meantime, Quinn and his eleven-year-old brother Jeff were giddy with excitement in the back seat.

"Go Mom, go!" They yelled their encouragement.

"I didn't know you could drive like *this*!" Jeff exclaimed.

Quinn laughed with glee, "This is so cool!"

I'm gonna ground him for 30 years; assuming we live through this.

Now we faced a problem. Up ahead the main road was under construction. There were orange cones everywhere and traffic looked backed up for blocks. The chances of us being able to turn right onto State Street before the angry hillbillies caught up were pretty slim.

"Start praying," I shouted. "Please Heavenly Father, please let us get in!" I kid you not, sunlight burst out from between some clouds when we approached the street, shining down on a small break in traffic. Without coming to a full stop I eased between the slowly moving cars, while our pursuers had to wait, honking their horn in frustration. I quickly turned into a Wendy's parking lot, glided in between two other vehicles, and we crouched down in our seats until it was safe to sit up and drive away. The boys were clapping each other on their backs and giving me high fives. It took me almost an hour to stop shaking.

This was my first, and hopefully last, high-speed chase. As I reflect though, as an only child growing up to be a mother of ten, it seems that my whole life has been a high-speed chase; pursuing a God I didn't come to know until after I'd already birthed nine babies. Life was getting increasingly challenging. Financial concerns weighed heavily on my mind. We were now relying solely on income that Scott brought in from teaching piano lessons. It seemed like something was always breaking down and in need of repair. We were barely scraping by, but I tried to count my blessings anyway.

One blessing I was thankful for was home schooling. Whenever we drove past the school bus stop on the way to the store or a family field trip, scantily-clad junior high school girls stood next to boys with huge baggy pants barely covering their rear ends. Some of them had cigarettes hanging out their mouths. *Little prostitutes and druggies*, I thought, somewhat uncharitably. *Where are their parents? Don't they care? What's wrong with these people? I'm so glad our kids aren't like that.* My smug views increased as time went by.

Every August or two I made a special trip up to Provo, Utah, to attend Brigham Young University's Education Week. There were so many topics to choose from. This particular time, one of the classes I chose to attend was about parenting teens. I settled into a good seat, taking out my notebook and pen. The speaker began with some inspirational thoughts and then told about her daughter who went astray. The girl began hanging out with the wrong crowd, and before too long started using drugs and became pregnant out of wedlock. The speaker went on to talk about parenting through difficult situations. I don't even remember what she said because I had tuned out. *How can she be up there telling people how to parent when her own daughter went off the deep end? She mustn't have been living the gospel. I wonder if they had Family Home Evening every week.*

I began to feel bad as those thoughts went through my mind. It was probably wrong to judge her like that. Maybe she did everything she could to live the gospel in her home, but her daughter was just a rebellious spirit from the preexistence or something…that was probably it. Still, I didn't go back to her class. Instead, I decided to listen to a successful speaker the next day, one whose children went on missions and got married in the temple. It was a great week as usual, and I came home feeling uplifted and strengthened.

I started implementing some of the things I learned, like following through with what I said, and how to hold children accountable for their actions. After grounding a couple of the kids for something, eight-year-old Curran asked, "Mom, what parenting book have you been reading? You need to stop."

I began feeling optimistic about our family and the direction it was heading. Then, one Sunday when it was my turn to teach in Relief Society, that optimism turned to despair. I made a quick trip home between meetings to get something I needed for the lesson. The phone rang just as I was heading out the door.

"Hello? I answered.

"Is this Quinn's mother?"

"Yes," I said slowly, wondering why someone would be calling me about my son.

"This is 'Bobby's' mom. Bobby has been selling and using drugs, and I'm not putting up with it any more. I'm getting the police involved and just wanted to warn you in advance in case he starts naming names."

"What do you mean? What does this have to do with Quinn?" By now I was alarmed.

"Quinn is one of his customers. I just thought you should know." *Click.*

I was stunned. Now it all made sense; Quinn's long hair (with a colored streak), the awful music by bands with weird names like Pearl Jam, Green Day, something Oysters or some type of shellfish, and I don't remember what else. All I knew was that it wasn't Janice Kapp Perry, Michael McLean, or the Tabernacle Choir he'd been listening to. Funny odors came from his room, but he insisted it was only incense. Things seemed to end up missing around the house, but I figured it was just my memory and had probably misplaced the small valuables myself. Quinn had become extremely moody and mean to his younger brothers and sister. I thought he was just going through a phase and that this was normal behavior for teens.

Devastated, I hung up the phone, and was barely able to compose myself when I got back to church. I couldn't make it through the Relief Society lesson without choking up and crying several times. I apologized, only saying that I had received some bad news just prior to getting there. After about the third time I started crying, Sister Baker got up and walked out of class. *I'm such a loser*, I thought. *I don't deserve to be up here.*

How I wished I could tell someone, to reach out to the sisters for advice and comfort, but how could I ever let them know? If they knew my son was on drugs, what would they think of our family? I'd never be able to teach again, let alone face them, because I just wasn't worthy enough. If only I had been more righteous this wouldn't be happening. Quinn wouldn't be going off the deep end. Our family was going to hell in a hand-basket and I felt utterly helpless to do anything about it.

The next few months were extremely stressful, as well as eye-opening. I found out through Quinn about other youth in the ward involved in drugs, drinking, and immorality. Tentatively, I put some feelers out to a few women I trusted, and learned their families were having the same struggles, only not just limited to the teens. One of the ladies from church, who was attending services less and less, abused drugs and alcohol. I thought the reason she was gone every few Sundays was because of work, but the real reason she didn't come was because she was hung over.

My balloon was burst. There was so much pain and suffering all around us, and I had been oblivious to it. Behind the smiling faces and handshakes at church were people with hurts, putting on "happy masks" so no one would suspect they weren't perfectly living the gospel. The whole ward was sick. The whole world was sick. How were any of us to ever going to make it to the Celestial Kingdom? Not just our family, but everyone in the Church. What about all the Christians and others in the world who were basically good people, but struggling with problems? How would anybody be able to make it back to Heavenly Father?

My attitude changed rather quickly. From that point on, whenever I drove past the school bus stop, I no longer looked with disdain at the students standing there, mentally calling them druggies and sluts. My heart broke for them, and even more so for their parents. "Heavenly Father," I would pray while driving past, "please help them. Please help their moms and dads. Please, oh please, help us all!"

A few paragraphs cannot adequately describe the challenges, heartache, and stress the next few years brought as our family came to terms with Quinn's drug addiction, but more will be said further on. Scott and I were drifting apart for a variety of reasons, and my now-chronic depression wasn't helping. Fortunately, Quinn's younger siblings weren't following in his footsteps. As they hit their teen years, they were more goofy than rebellious. One never knew what to expect from them.

CHAPTER 12

Raising Teens, Pulling Teeth, and Pole Dancing

This is insane! Why is this happening to me? What did I do?

—Neo, The Matrix

I never thought taking the kids to get their wisdom teeth removed would be so daunting.

The doctor warned Tristan with a smile, "Now when you are on this medication, you may feel an urge to tell the truth or lose your inhibitions."

After Tristan woke up, the nurse called me back to sit with him in the recovery room. Goofy smiles. Okay, I can deal with that. Giggles. Okay, giggles are tolerable. Then confession; "Mom, you know what I really want to do?"

"No son, tell me." I patted his hand.

"Pole dance."

"Okaaaay, that's nice. So, how do you feel," I asked, changing the subject, wondering how my upright Mormon son even knew what pole dancing was.

"I feel like pole dancing." He began to gyrate in the chair.

"Jeff!" I called, "Jeff, can you come in here please?" Jeff had come for the ride. I'm glad I had backup! It started to feel warm in the room.

"Ooh, baby!" Tristan tried to get out of the recliner. "La, la, la! Cha, cha, cha, yeah!"

Beads of sweat now forming on my palms. "Jeff! Can you do something?" I pleaded when he came into the room. This was so embarrassing. What if all the people in the waiting room were listening? I didn't want them all to think my son was a closet pervert. *I'm under control. I'm under control. I can deal with this.*

Jeff pushed Tristan gently back into the chair. "Hey, bro, cool it."

"Cha, cha, cha, ooh la la," was the response.

A nurse walked by, raising her eyebrows.

"I bet pole dancers make good money." Tristan began calculating the potential income.

"They probably do," I answered, "but you really need to sit still so your mouth doesn't bleed."

"Yeah, okay, Mom." He closed his eyes. No movement. A minute passed. My heart rate began to slow again. A sigh of relief escaped me.

"You know, I could be a good pole dancer." His gyrations began again.

Thump-thump, thump-thump, thump-thump. Blood pressure rising. Arm-pits sweating. *How much longer do we need to be here?* It must have been an hour already. I looked at my watch; fifteen minutes.

The nurse came by and smiled, "So how's he..."

"*Fine!* Fine." I cut her off a little too quickly. "Just fine, thank you." She tilted her head, shrugged, and moved on.

"Oooh baby, ooh baby, la la la..."

"Bro, come on, you're upsetting mom. You can dance when we get home," Jeff soothed.

"Okay," Nurse Cheery Cheeks popped in. "You're free to go."

I bolted up from the chair.

"Do you need any help?" She smiled.

"No," I answered too quickly, cutting her off again. "No." *Calm down, act casual.* "No. That's kind of you. We're fine, really."

I took one of Tristan's arms and Jeff took the other. The nurse shrugged and opened the door for us. We walked down the sidewalk leading away from the office, Tristan's hips swinging like he was Elvis Presley and Tom Jones rolled up into one. I felt the nurse's shocked eyes burning into my back. We turned the corner.

"Why don't you get the van, Mom, while I help Tristan walk?" Jeff swung Tristan's arm over his shoulder and supported him around the waist. They looked more like dancing partners than anything else.

"Great idea," I replied, starting off across the parking lot.

"Hey! Hey!" Tristan shouted. I turned to see an older couple walking to their car. "Hey, you wanna dance? Whooo yeah, whooo yeah!" Tristan shouted at them, swaying like a drunkard, trying to break away from his brother's grasp. I broke into a jog, head down, with embarrassment brightening my cheeks.

The couple stood watching as Tristan and Jeff headed toward the van where I was standing. *Go away. Just go away,* I silently willed the nosy old people.

"He's sick! He's not himself!" I shouted, getting in and sliding down in the front seat. The man gripped his wife's elbow and led her to their car. Jeff coaxed Tristan into the front seat and strapped him in, where he twisted and turned to imaginary music. At every red light I worried he would jump out and twirl around the nearest light pole. I broke the speed limit all the way home. We got Tristan into bed where he slept soundly for the next several hours. He didn't remember a thing, but I remembered every humiliating detail.

Jeff had to have all his wisdom teeth out just before Christmas. I took him to the same doctor that Tristan had gone to. No one else went with us and I didn't think to ask. Big mistake.

"He did really well," the nurse told me, "you can come back and sit with him in recovery. I sat down next to him. Jeff looked at me groggily and tried to get up.

"You need to lie back down, Jeff."

"Why?"

"Because they want you to rest for a few minutes before we leave, so the anesthesia wears off a little."

"I feel fine. Why can't we go now?" Jeff tried getting up again.

"Jeff, just lay there for a few minutes. We'll leave when they tell us we can."

"I feel fine. When can I take this gauze out of my mouth?" Jeff asked, the muffled words trying to escape through a stuffed orifice.

The nurse poked her head in. "You need to stop talking and just relax. You're going to prolong the bleeding."

"See?" I said, "You're supposed to rest."

"Well, I don't need to. I can get up. I feel fine. The stuff they gave me hasn't affected me." He bolted upright in the chair.

"Jeff! Just sit down and close your eyes!" I was beginning to feel uncomfortable. Déja Vu all over again.

Jeff jumped out the chair, swayed a bit like a sapling in a stiff spring breeze, and smiled at me triumphantly. "See? I'm fine. Watch this!" Gee, I could hardly wait. At least he wasn't pole dancing. He threw himself down onto the floor, dazed from the sudden drop in elevation, and paused to catch his breath. Then he began doing push-ups.

"Jeff, please get up," I pleaded.

"Two…three…four…" Jeff huffed.

Lord, help me! I put my head down pretending to read the book I brought, trying to be oblivious to what was happening. Out of my peripheral vision I saw the nurse walk by, back up, and do a double-take.

"Mr. Crookston!" she scolded, "Get in that chair right now!" She grabbed him by the arm and forced him into the chair. "You're bleeding!" Jeff lowered his head sheepishly while the nurse glared at me.

"I-I couldn't control him," I stammered, "He wouldn't listen to me."

The nurse removed the blood-soaked gauze and replaced it with fresh dry packs. "Sit!" she commanded. "Don't you *dare* get up."

Humiliation began enveloping me like a shockwave, starting at the crown of my head and rapidly spreading, traveling down to my toes. *How much longer?* I looked at my watch. Eons seemed to drag by, but it had only been two minutes since the last time I looked.

After what felt like an eternity the nurse came in and said we could go. Sweet deliverance! We made it out to the van and began the drive home. Jeff began to squirm. He was eyeballing the door. I accelerated. *Okay light, stay green, stay green, no! Don't turn red. No! Oh, man!*

"Jeff," I said as casually as I could, "why don't you put your seatbelt on? I'd hate to get stopped." I braced myself for resistance, but to my surprise, Jeff complied.

"Can we stop at Horlacher's house? I need to get my glasses," he asked.

"Maybe we should just go home. I'll pick them up later," I offered.

"But it's right on the way home."

"Well…I don't know," I was uncertain as to the wisdom of stopping anywhere besides home. After some badgering on Jeff's part, I consented to stop. "Just stay in the van. Don't move. Just stay right here. I'll go to the door." I got out of the van and walked quickly to the front door, glancing over my shoulder every two seconds. Jeff was actually behaving. No one answered my repeated knocks and doorbell ringing. I wrote a note on the back of our business card and stuck it in the doorjamb.

"They weren't home so I left a note about your glasses," I explained, about to put the van in reverse. Jeff opened the door and sprang out.

"Wait! What are you doing?" I cried.

"I'll just go in and get them," Jeff shouted to me as he reached for their doorknob.

"Jeff, just get in the van."

Jeff went to the garage and tried the combination lock. "I can just go in through their garage." It didn't work. He walked up to the side gate and was about to scale it.

"*What are you doing?*" I demanded.

"Going into the backyard. Their back door might be unlocked."

"What if there's a dog? He'll rip out your remaining teeth!" I began to panic.

"There's no dog," Jeff reassured me.

"Jeff, don't you dare climb that wall," I yelled. "Get in the van *right now* or you're in big trouble, mister!"

Jeff stood motionless, teetering on the brink of indecision. He must have seen the wild look in my eyes and decided to obey his half-crazed mother. He got into the van, closed the door, and asked, "What's the problem?

"The problem is called 'breaking and entering,' and it's against the law."

"It's just entering, not breaking" he rationalized, as he got back into the van. "I'm sure they wouldn't mind."

By this time we were barreling down the road toward home, with me silently praying the traffic signals would be favorable. *Stay green, stay green. Please don't turn. Oh, man! Yellow's okay, I can make it, I can make it. Whoops! Oh well.*

"So how'd it go?" Scott inquired as I came in the door.

"Don't ask," I replied, "Don't even go there."

Jeff slept soundly for the next several hours and awoke remembering bits and pieces. I, however, remembered every humiliating detail.

Summer was the next one needing her wisdom teeth pulled. "Mom, you're going to take me to the oral surgeon on Thursday, right?"

"No, I'm going to ask dad to."

"*What?*" Summer exclaimed, "I don't want Daddy to take me. I want *you* to take me."

"Sorry, I can't. I just can't."

Summer raised her eyebrows, questioning.

"Look," I explained, "I don't want to know your secret fantasies; I don't want to be witness to some macho I-Can-Do-Anything stuff. I don't want to see the female version of it either; 'I Am Woman, Hear Me Roar.' I can't do it. I won't do it."

"But if I do anything embarrassing, I don't want Daddy to be there."

"Oh, so torture your poor mother? No. Sorry. No-can-do."

As it turned out, Scott had a music seminar to attend that morning. How convenient. The task fell upon me once again to accompany one of our kids to the oral surgeon's office. I'm sure we had made quite a reputation for ourselves by then. They probably had hidden cameras so they could watch the show from an adjacent room while eating popcorn and passing around O'Doule's.

The morning of the surgery, Summer took out a pad of paper on way to the office. "Okay," she said, as she began writing a vow. "I will not dance, do push-ups, be mean, or get up out of the chair. What else?"

"Or be silly?" I asked.

"Silly is okay, isn't it, Mom?"

"I don't know, Summer. I don't know if I can handle silly. Just try to sit there and rest after you wake up. Just sit quietly until it's time to go."

We made chitchat with the nurse while waiting for the doctor, recounting the past.

"I remember," the nurse mused.

"I couldn't control them," I said, defending myself.

"Males are little more aggressive when they are under the effects of this medication."

That was comforting to hear. Maybe Summer wouldn't be so bad. I held her hand until the doctor administered the sodium brevitol and Summer's eyes rolled back in their sockets. Settling comfortably on a couch with a book in the lobby, I awaited (with some anxiety) the call to come back into the recovery room. About twenty minutes later I was being ushered into the back of the office.

Summer lounged on a recliner, looking like a drunken lush; head swaying, red-eyed, and goofy.

"So," I ventured, "how are you feeling?" *Brace yourself. Here it comes.*

"Mymowthithdwy."

"Excuse me?"

"Dwy.Mowthithdwy," she mumbled, cheeks bulging with bloody gauze.

"I'm sorry, I don't understand."

"Wherahsmypen?" Summer fumbled around for her pocket, pulled out a ballpoint and started writing on her hand.

"Don't do that. Don't write on your hand."

Summer stuck her tongue out and pulled at it. "Ithsodwy, feel it. Do you underthand me?"

"Yes, yes, I understand you. Your mouth is dry, and no, I don't want to feel your tongue."

"Look. Thee? Ehhh, ahhh" she began poking at the roof of her mouth.

"I'm sure you can drink something when we get home. Now just lie still and rest." I instructed.

"Look! Theemymowth? Feelit. Ith dwy."

"Don't talk. Talking is making your mouth dry. Just rest."

More talk. More tongue clawing. More writing scribbles on a scrap of paper. More of my pleading for silence.

"I'm behaving" Summer said. "I'm not doingph anyfing I wote down I wouldn't do."

"Can you add no talking? You're talking too much. You're making yourself bleed more."

"Get the nuth. I wan wata."

"You can't have any now."

"Did I take my wath outta my pocket?"

"Your watch was in your hand when I came in here," I informed her.

"*I* didn't thake it out. Did *thay* go in my pocket?"

"I don't know. It doesn't matter. Now just be quiet."

"My mowth ith so dwy. Did I take my wath outta my pocket?"

And so it went, *all* the way out to the van. *All* the way home. Yackety-smackety, blah, blah, blah, chit chit chit, chat chat chat, *non*-stop.

"Your breath reeks, Summer, will you *please* stop talking?"

"Jeff's bweath thmelled the thame way. My mowth tasth like old tuna fish."

"Well it smells like tuna fish; tuna that went through a shark's digestive tract." I turned the vent on full blast.

"Ithn't that cold? Aren't you freething? Whath ah those fumes?" Summer asked, almost coherently.

"I would rather breathe that truck's cold exhaust then smell your breath. Now close your pie hole and give it a rest," I ordered, feeling light-headed from carbon monoxide pouring into the van through the air vents.

I'd like to say we drove home in silence, but no such luck. Summer stopped talking only long enough to catch her breath or claw at her tongue. Unlike her brothers, she did *not* sleep for hours, but talked and complained till I lost track of time. I was grateful for the privilege of leaving home to get her prescriptions filled. I looked for a busy pharmacy, a *very busy* pharmacy, and returned a couple hours later to the sound of her voice wafting throughout the house. Perhaps the pain meds would make her drowsy; if not, perhaps they would ease *my* pain.

After several days we fell back into the machinations of routine family life once again. Perhaps things would be more peaceful during the next year. Hopefully, getting our kids to be normal wouldn't be like pulling teeth.

CHAPTER 13

Those Pesky Born-Again Christians

I know this steak doesn't exist. I know that when I put it in my mouth, the Matrix is telling my brain that it is juicy and delicious. After nine years, you know what I realize? [Takes a bite of steak] Ignorance is bliss.

—Cypher, The Matrix

Blessings in disguise usually reveal themselves after the fact. After the disappointment, heartbreak, or failure, you can often look back and see how things actually worked out for the best. Our income had dwindled, the debts stacked up, and before we knew it we had to move again after seven years in the big gray house with bright blue trim. I was actually glad to be leaving the neighborhood, as there were too many painful memories there and way too much anxiety.

I'm sure the people across the street were happy to see us go. The feelings were mutual. I was more than happy to be out from under their condescending noses and mettlesome ways. The "Stott's" never really liked us, especially after finding out we were Mormons. But then again, they didn't appear to really like anyone except for the people next-door to them and the ones next to us. All three families had something in common; they were "Born-Again Christians," whatever *that* meant. At first I saw it as a "missionary opportunity." Since they already believed in God it seemed like the ideal situation. All we would have to do is move them from well-meaning-but-corrupted-Christendom to the One True Church restored by the prophet Joseph Smith.

It didn't quite work that way. No matter how many times I invited them to ward functions, or asked the ladies if they would like to come to Homemaking Meeting (held once a month), they always had an excuse for not going. Not only that, but the people next door *never, ever* let their two sons come into our house, and they rarely let any of our kids into theirs. I wondered if they had something against big families, but after a while I came to the conclusion they had something against Mormons.

My daughter Summer became best friends with the girl cattycorner to us, and often spent hours talking to her mother about religion. Her friend Sarah would plead, "Come on, Summer! Can we play now?" Summer would finally pull herself away from their kitchen table and play dolls or some game, then later come home and tell me all about the conversations she had with Kristy, Sarah's mom. Summer told her all about our church and Joseph Smith and why we still needed prophets today. Everything she learned in Primary, Sunday school, and our own Family Home Evenings (FHE) she repeated to Kristy.

"I don't know, Summy. There's just something wrong about it. I can't explain why. I just don't think we need to work for our salvation." I actually thought the conversations were good for Summer because it helped her learn to share the gospel and it also planted seeds. Maybe one day Kristy would get baptized and become a Mormon. I think if Kristy had really known how to defend her Christian faith, I wouldn't have felt so comfortable with Summer spending so much time there.

The Stott's were a different breed altogether. They gained a reputation for being the self-appointed neighborhood police. If someone was watering their lawn between 11 a.m. and 7 p.m. from June through August, Mrs. Stott would promptly call the water district to report the homeowner for breaking water conservation regulations. If someone's dog barked too much they would call animal control (even though their own obnoxious little ankle-biter was outside barking every morning at 4 a.m.). If someone's toddler ran outside in diapers, you could rest assured Child Protective Services became involved due to the Stott's interference.

I tried making conversation about the Lord with the neighbors and the Stott's whenever the opportunity arose, just to find something in common with them to let them see that we were people of faith too. It didn't matter. They never warmed up to us, and I felt like we were pariahs. Well, if that's what Christians were like, I wanted little to do with them.

Our Church leaders were right; according to Scripture we, as Mormons, would be considered a "peculiar people" and could expect to not be accepted or understood by the world. I thought about the prophecy in the book of Daniel in the Bible that foretold of a stone cut without hands that became a great mountain that filled the earth. That was a prophecy about the LDS Church; our gospel. Despite persecution or disdain by Gentiles (non-Mormons), one day Mormonism would be vindicated. Jesus Christ would return to the earth and rule from the New Jerusalem in Jackson County, Missouri. Then, everyone in the world would know that the Mormons were right after all. Dr. Walter Martin already found out the hard way that Mormonism was true.

I was sad for Dr. Martin in a way. He passed away from a heart attack in 1989. Now he was in spirit prison, but hopefully would have the chance to accept the gospel, even though it was too late for him to make it to the Celestial Kingdom. Walter Martin was known as "The Bible Answer Man," and had a daily radio program. I could never stand listening to him, but Scott often came home to tell me what vitriol Walter had spewed out that day. Interestingly, when Scott was working graveyard shifts as a dishwasher at the Stardust Hotel & Casino, the only radio station that came in clearly enough to be heard was the Christian radio station that carried the Bible Answer Man program.

The problem was that Dr. Martin got the facts right, but the way he reported them made Mormonism look bad. For instance, he would say how Mormons believed that God the Father came down to earth and had sex with Mary, the mother of Jesus, and how it amounted to incest, since she was his spirit daughter. I supposed technically that was true; according to the writings of several LDS prophets and apostles, Heavenly Father did have physical relations with Mary, who was one of his spiritual wives as well as a daughter, but Dr. Martin stated it in such an inflammatory way as to make it sound vulgar and disgusting.

When Scott first started listening, he thought Martin was a "liar, liar" with his "eternal pants on fire." Scott got so upset, that he became determined to prove the man wrong. However, every reference Martin gave checked out accurately. Scott's anger turned to interest. He began buying "anti-Mormon literature" in used bookstores, ostensibly for research. He still fervently believed the Church was true, but was set on becoming familiar with the arguments against Mormonism so he could refute them. That mindset lasted until he found a book on one of his "pokey-stick" excursions. Lying in a dumpster on top of a pile of clothing was a book by Charles Larson called *By His Own Hand Upon Papyrus*.

Scott began reading the book and couldn't put it down. For three days in a row he told me what he had read that day. I was shaken up by it. The book basically told about the discovery of the papyrus that Joseph Smith translated from for the Book of Abraham in the Pearl of Great Price, which Latter-day Saints consider to be Scripture.

July 3, 1835, Mr. Michael H. Chandler and his traveling mummy exhibition rolled through Kirtland, Ohio. His exhibit contained four mummies, two rolls of papyrus, and "two or three other small pieces of papyrus, with astronomical calculations, epitaphs, &c. [sic]."[1] Chandler heard that Smith had the gift of translation and could decipher Egyptian characters. The Church bought the mummies and papyrus from Mr. Chandler for about $2,400 and Joseph commenced translating the scrolls right away.

Amazingly, Joseph said one of the scrolls of papyri was inscribed by the Old Testament patriarch Abraham himself. The other scroll was written on by Abraham's descendent, Joseph, son of Jacob and Rachel. Once the translation was complete, it was published in 1842 in the Church's *Times and Seasons* as the "Book of Abraham," later becoming part of Mormon Scripture known as *The Pearl of Great Price*.

In the book Scott found, the author, Charles Larson, argued that the very same papyrus Joseph Smith used for his translation was found in some basement somewhere and scholars determined that the papyrus scrolls were much more recent than the time of Abraham. I didn't know what else the book said because I didn't want to hear any more about it. For three days I was extremely distraught. All I could think about was what it would mean if the Church wasn't true. I remember sitting in the car in the grocery store parking lot crying, trying to compose myself before going shopping.

"Heaven Father," I prayed, "what if Joseph Smith got it all wrong? What would we do? What should I do? What about the kids? If the Church isn't true…I don't even want to think about it." I thought about all the good feelings I had about the Church, and the many spiritual experiences I had over the years. Didn't that prove the Church was true? What about the peace I felt in the Celestial Room of the temple? Of course the Church was true. Of course! I breathed a sigh of relief, dried my tears, bought some groceries (and chocolate) and went home.

After the kids got settled down for the night, Scott and I went on our usual evening walk around the block.

"Scott, I don't want you to tell me anymore about that book. Deep inside I just know the Church is true. When I think about it *not* being true, I feel all agitated and upset. That's probably the Spirit telling me not to listen to anti-Mormon stuff."

"Okay. I won't tell you about what I'm reading," Scott promised.

"I don't want you telling any of this to the kids either. They're too young and impressionable. What if you shake their testimonies and the Church really *is* true, and they go astray, we'll never all make it to the Celestial Kingdom? If you want to go to hell that's your business, but you're not taking me and the kids with you."

"I'll keep my doubts to myself," he assured me.

The Stott's, the neighbors, and the other people across the street could think whatever they wanted about us. We had the true gospel, and ultimately that was all that mattered. One day, all of them, along with the late Dr. Walter Martin, would know once and for all that Mormonism was true, and they'll ask living Mormons to do temple work in their behalf so they can progress eternally.

Actually, maybe it wouldn't take that long for our neighbors to know the Mormon Church was true. Church President Gordon B. Hinckley was going to be interviewed on Larry King Live. He'll tell the whole world that the Church is true and that Joseph Smith was a real prophet of God. He'll use this rare interview, watched by millions of people, as a missionary opportunity to spread the gospel. I could hardly wait.

---

1. History of the Church, Vol. 2, 1976, 349

CHAPTER 14

From PR Man to Prophet

Whatever you think you know about this man is irrelevant... He is considered by many authorities to be the most dangerous man alive.

—Agent Smith, The Matrix

Bruce Green, our friend and director of Bluth Chorale, got the TV out of the church library and rolled it on its cart into the chapel where we were rehearsing. We were all so excited. The "stand" (area up behind the podium where all the choir seats are) was buzzing with chatter and anticipation as we waited for "60 Minutes"[1] to come on. All voices fell to a hush as the rare interview, airing April 1996, with Church President Gordon B. Hinckley started. We wondered what the prophet would tell the world.

He began by telling about Joseph Smith, and how God and Jesus appeared to him in the woods near his home when he was 14 years old. Correspondent Mike Wallace asked President Hinckley about the "very strict health code" (known to us as the Word of Wisdom), clarifying, "No alcohol, no tobacco, no coffee, no tea, not even caffeinated soft drinks...," to which the prophet responded, "That's right." Scott and I looked at each other from the tenor and alto sections and nodded.

Ha! We were vindicated. You see, it was our belief that whatever the prophets taught needed to be followed, even if something wasn't specifically spelled out. In this case, the "letter of the law," Section 89 of the *Doctrine & Covenants*, instructed us to abstain from hot drinks, referring to tea and coffee. Church leaders later explained that tea and coffee were prohibited because of the detrimental effects of caffeine. So, it naturally followed that the "spirit of the law" in the Word of Wisdom would include cola-drinks or soft drinks containing caffeine. Coca-cola wasn't mentioned in D&C 89 simply because it didn't exist when the revelation was given. We had close friends who regularly drank caffeine soda and justified it by saying that since it wasn't spelled out in the Word of Wisdom, it therefore was not a sin. We replied that cocaine wasn't mentioned in the Word of Wisdom either, but they wouldn't think of using that. Now we could look our LDS friends in the eye and tell them we heard it straight from President Hinckley himself.

Later in the interview Mike Wallace said, "From 1830 to 1978...blacks could not become priests in the Mormon Church, right?"

"That's correct," President Hinckley answered.

"Why?"

"Because the leaders of the Church at that time interpreted that doctrine that way," President Hinckley said.

Mike stated, "Church policy had it that blacks had the mark of Cain. Brigham Young said, 'Cain slew his brother and the Lord put a mark upon him, which is the flat nose and black skin.'"

President Hinckley told him, "It's behind us. Look, that's behind us. Don't worry about those little flicks of history."

Blacks being denied the priesthood were "little flicks of history?" His answer kind of troubled Scott and me because it wasn't exactly honest; or at least it wasn't completely true. While I felt uncomfortable about the doctrine—feeling bad for black people, especially since I knew two wonderful black Mormon men who were stalwart, faithful members of the Church before they could even hold the priesthood—we couldn't get around it. The fact was, that's what the Lord revealed to Brigham Young and other prophets, so whether we liked the doctrine or not, who were we to argue with God?

President Hinckley made it sound like the teaching was some passing fad. On the other hand, we had to admit it was rather clever how our prophet avoided addressing the issue and bringing embarrassment to the Church. After all, it was okay to be only half-truthful in order to protect the gospel, right? We wouldn't want to "cast pearls before swine."

Over all, the *60 Minutes* interview went well. We were proud to be members of the One True Church. We thought it was pretty cool how the Lord had groomed Gordon B. Hinckley to one day become prophet by giving him an education in public relations, knowing in advance he would someday represent the Church on TV.

The following year some more exciting developments with the Church occurred. The LDS Church and President Hinckley were featured on the cover of TIME Magazine. The article's title, *Kingdom Come*, appeared in the August 4, 1997 issue. The article was pretty accurate, and for the most part cast Mormonism in a favorable light. There was only one thing that shocked and dismayed us. One part of the article said;

> On whether his church still holds that God the Father was once a man, he [President Hinckley] sounded uncertain, "I don't know that we teach it. I don't know that we emphasize it... I understand the philosophical background behind it, but I don't know a lot about it, and I don't think others know a lot about it."[2]

It appeared that President Hinckley lied. I couldn't understand it. I was proud of that unique doctrine; the fact that Heavenly Father was once like us on some other world—perhaps eons ago—and went through the same kinds of struggles as we do. It was a comforting thought. Why would the prophet lie about it? It was very much a part of Mormon teachings. True, we didn't hear about it over the pulpit frequently, but it could be found in the writings and teachings of LDS prophets and apostles from the time of Joseph Smith to the present. In fact, Joseph himself declared;

> You will then know that I am His servant; for I speak as one having authority. I will go back to the beginning before the world was, to show what kind of a being God is. What sort of a being was God in the beginning? ...God himself was once as we are now, and is an exalted man, and sits enthroned in yonder heavens! That is the great secret.[3]

He said that it was necessary for us to understand the character and nature of God;

> ...I am going to tell you how God came to be God. We have imagined and supposed that God was God from all eternity. I will refute that idea, and take away the veil, so that you may see...He was once a man like us; yea, that God himself, the Father of us all, dwelt on an earth, the same as Jesus Christ Himself did; and I will show it from the Bible.[4]

Joseph was quite explicit when he taught;

> Here, then, is eternal life—to know the only wise and true
> God; and you have got to learn how to be gods yourselves, and to
> be kings and priests to God, the same as all gods have done before
> you, namely, by going from one small degree to another, and from
> a small capacity to a great one; from grace to grace, from exaltation
> to exaltation, until you attain to the resurrection of the dead, and
> are able to dwell in everlasting burnings, and to sit in glory, as do
> those who sit enthroned in everlasting power.[5]

In our newest (at the time) Priesthood and Relief Society Study Guide for
1997, *Teachings of the Presidents of the Church: Brigham Young*, page 29 records;

> [President Brigham Young] taught further that God the Fa-
> ther was once a man on another planet who "passed the ordeals we
> are now passing trough; he has received an experience, has suffered
> and enjoyed, and knows all that we know regarding the toils, suffer-
> ings, life and death of this mortality."[6]

Furthermore, the manual goes on to teach, "Some would have us believe that
God is present everywhere. It is not so."[7]

President Hinckley's dishonesty continued to trouble me, but I kept telling
myself there had to be a good explanation. The explanation came over the pulpit
by President Hinckley himself in a General Conference address two months after the TIME interview was published. In his talk entitled *Drawing Nearer to the
Lord*, President Hinckley stated;

> I personally have been much quoted, and in a few instances
> misquoted and misunderstood. I think that's to be expected. None
> of you need worry because you read something that was incom-
> pletely reported. You need not worry that I do not understand
> some matters of doctrine. I think I understand them thoroughly,
> and it is unfortunate that the reporting may not make this clear.[8]

I was relieved. Apparently, the prophet was misquoted. The Church is true.
Nothing to worry about, or was there?

Once again President Hinckley was on Larry King Live about a year later.
The program aired in September of 1998. The interview seemed to be focused
as much on politics and sports as on religion. Larry kept going back to questions

about U.S. President Bill Clinton's moral failure, to which President Hinckley kept replying that while we should forgive, there should be some accountability in place for someone holding the highest office in the land. I wished Larry would get off politics and ask questions about the gospel.

He brought up the issue of polygamy and "fundamentalist Mormons." President Hinckley told him that polygamy was in the past and there's no such thing as fundamentalist Mormons, which wasn't quite true, at least not fully. Even though polygamy is not practiced by the main LDS Church currently, it's still a part of our doctrines and essential to life in the Celestial Kingdom (which I was *not* looking forward to, I might add). And as far as the "Fundamentalists" go, even though they don't represent the Church and even though they have gone astray, they *do* exist. Ignoring them, denying them, or making up some other name for them didn't keep them from being what they were; groups of people trying to live the gospel the way it was taught by Joseph Smith and Brigham Young; fundamentalists getting back to the fundamentals of original Mormonism.

I later came across a transcript of the TIME magazine interview, which showed that President Hinckley was *not* quoted out of context. Not only was he less than forthright with TIME, but it would seem with Church members as well. But again, a good explanation was coming.

My kids and I went to Idaho for the summer to spend time with Scott's sister Kay and her husband Joseph. As was always the case when visiting relatives, we stayed up late many nights to have gospel discussions. We also attended several get-togethers with like-minded Church members to talk about each other's' experiences and the role of Mormonism in End Times prophecy.

One night I expressed my concerns about President Hinckley to Joseph and asked him what his thoughts were, "Do you think President Hinckley is a fallen prophet?"

"Tracy, you can't fall from someplace you've never been. The Church has been out of order since after Joseph Smith. We've had several presidents of the Church who have been inspired, but they're not prophets. But don't let it worry you. When the Lord returns he will 'clean house' and set everything back in order."

"How can this be?" I asked, wide-eyed in attention. "I thought Ezra Taft Benson and Brigham Young said the Lord would never let a prophet lead us astray, and that even if he *is* wrong, we'll be blessed for obeying what he says."[9]

"Well," Joseph replied, "the Church is in apostasy, and has been ever since the time of Joseph Smith. Brigham Young made the statement that he had never seen the face of the Lord. Heber J. Grant said that too. You know, there isn't one president of the Church who can admit they've seen the face of the Lord since Joseph Smith. We haven't had a prophet, seer, and revelator, even though we sustain them as such. President Hinckley cannot have fallen from some position he's never held."

"What does that mean then?" I asked, quite disturbed. "Does this mean we haven't really been led by prophets?"

"Some of them have been inspired in relevance to their calling, but not in the sense that they are prophets as Joseph Smith was, or Moses or Isaiah."

"But I don't get it. This is the Lord's Church. How could it possibly be in shambles?"

"The Church has been under condemnation since 1832," Joseph explained. "It says that in section 84 of the Doctrine & Covenants. President Benson; he was very inspired—directed by the Spirit just like you and I could be—relevant to his calling. He said in his famous Book of Mormon conference address—I think it was 1986—that the Church was still under condemnation. No president of the Church has ever said otherwise. So the Church is *still* under condemnation, we still have a preparatory gospel, the Lord's removed a lot of things from us, and we do not have the fullness; the fullness is a personal thing. We do not get it through the Church."

"But," I started to object.

"No, wait. This is still the Lord's Church, but it's out of order. Section 112 tells about calamities in the End Times, and the Lord says 'On my house shall it begin and from my house shall it go forth.' So what is his house?"

"I don't know; the Church?" I ventured.

"It's his people. He can't tell other people to go clean their house when his own house is out of order, so all this vengeance and the Day of Wrath are going to start on his house. Why? Because his house is wicked. Here, let's read D&C 112, verses 24 through 27;

> "24. Behold, vengeance cometh speedily upon the inhabitants of the earth, a day of wrath, a day of burning, a day of desolation, of weeping, of morning, and of lamentation; and as a whirlwind it will come upon all the face of the earth, saith the Lord.
>
> 25. An upon my house shall it begin, and from my house shall it go forth, saith the Lord;
>
> 26. First among those among you, saith the Lord, who have professed to know my name and have not known me, and have blasphemed against me in the midst of my house, saith the Lord.

27. Therefore, see to it that ye trouble not yourselves concerning the affairs of my church in this place, saith the Lord."

My brother-in-law continued, "My own judgment and interpretation of that is; we've got those that claim to be apostles and prophets in the Church that are not, allowing people to believe they've seen the Lord and know him, but they don't. And he's going to clean house. Yet, this is still the Lord's Church and he knows what's going on, so you don't have to worry."

What Joseph said kind of made sense, but then again it didn't. Did that mean the Church is true but the leaders are not? Or the gospel is true but the Church is not? Why did the Lord go through all that trouble to restore the gospel through Joseph Smith if the Church was going to go into apostasy after he was killed? It was too much to think about and try to figure out. I decided to just put it on a mental shelf and wait for the Lord to clean house.

---

1. Details of the interview can be found on CBSnews.com; http://www.cbsnews.com/2100-18560_162-3775068.html?pageNum=2&tag=contentMain;contentBody
2. Richard Ostling, Kingdom Come. *Time Magazine, August 4, 1997, p. 56.*
3. Excerpts from a reprint of the King Follett sermon, retrieved from http://www.lds.org/ensign/print/1971/04/the-king-follett-sermon?lang=eng&clang=eng
4. Ibid
5. Ibid
6. Teachings of the Presidents of the Church: Brigham Young, *Knowing and Honoring the Godhead*, Chapter 4, (The Church of Jesus Christ of Latter-day Saints: Salt Lake City, UT, 1997) 29.
7. Ibid
8. Gordon B. Hinckley, Drawing Nearer to the Lord. Ensign Magazine. October 1997. Retrieved from https://www.lds.org/general-conference/1997/10/drawing-nearer-to-the-lord?lang=eng
9. "God will not permit me, or any other President who holds the keys, to intentionally lead you astray." Gospel Principles, Prophets of God. Chapter 9, (The Church of Jesus Christ of Latter-day Saints: Salt Lake City: UT) 48.

CHAPTER 15

Like an Outsider Looking In

Perhaps we are asking the wrong questions.

—Agent Brown, The Matrix

Waiting for the Lord to "clean house" wasn't going to be easy. How would we know if we were being deceived or not if even some of our prophets could be in error? And if the prophets were getting revelation the same way the average church member did—by impressions, feelings, and the "still, small voice"—then what was the point in having prophets?

How come the still, small voice of the Spirit seems to tell some people one thing and other people something contradictory? How were we to know what was true? Brigham Young taught that all truth belongs to the LDS Church and that we should accept truth no matter where it is found, even in the realms of science and philosophy.[1]

All I wanted was for my family to make it to the Celestial Kingdom. All the Mormons I really respected and admired seemed to have a direct hotline to the Holy Ghost. My friend and singing teacher, Pat, always seemed to get revelation and promptings from the Spirit, usually, she told me, while in the shower or bathroom. I never got revelations in the bathroom. The only revelation I got in the bathroom was that I should probably eat more roughage.

During a singing lesson Pat would often pause, cock her head to one side as if she was listening to something, and mumble, "Now *that's* interesting…" I'd ask her what was so interesting, and she'd reply that the Spirit just told her maybe she should use this or that vocal technique to help increase my range or smooth out a break in my voice.

Pat wasn't the only one who regularly heard from the Spirit. I had other friends who would tell me they were praying and got impressions from the Holy Ghost, or they went to the temple and had some wonderful revelation, or could sense the presence of a departed relative or the spirit of the person they went through the temple for. While I felt peaceful at the temple (especially when falling asleep during the endowment session) (Ok, look. Not to say it was boring or anything, but when you have little children running you ragged at home and you're up nursing a baby several times a night, it's very easy to drift off into a sound slumber in the middle of the endowment movie. Just try to sit with a friend so they can nudge you at the appropriate time), I never got visitations from spirits (a.k.a. "I see dead people," reminiscent of the movie *The Sixth Sense*). Maybe because I was sleeping…hmmm…now that's a thought. But I digress.

I prayed and fasted to be closer to the Spirit and to recognize its promptings more. I remembered Brother Kirby from the 10th Ward in the North Stake. He was amazing. Brother Kirby was such a likable, good-natured guy. He was always saying things like, "I was driving home from work and the Spirit said, 'Yo, Kirby! You need to take some milk over to Sister So-and-so.'" And he would take milk to the person's house and she would say how they had no milk for the children and no money to buy any. I envied people like that. Oh, not the people with no milk and no money. Been there, done that. I mean the people who had a personal visit from the Holy Ghost. The Spirit never said to me, "Yo, Tracy!" But here was Brother Kirby, practically on a first-name basis with the Godhead. What was wrong with me? Brother Kirby, Carl and LeAnne, Bob and Lynn, and other friends all explained to me many times that one had to "practice" listening to the Still Small Voice. So I tried my best.

One morning I was leaving the house to run errands. As I got around the corner the thought came that I should go back and check the gate to make sure it was locked. At that time our two little boys enjoyed sneaking out the door, standing on a tot chair, and unlatching the gate to play in the front yard in diapers or naked, as the mood suited them. I didn't remember locking the gate, and since that very morning while praying I told Heavenly Father I wanted to learn to recognize the "still, small voice," I decided to go back and check just in case my thought was a prompting of the Spirit.

Putting the gear shift in park and leaving the car running, I sprinted across the lawn to check the latch. About halfway there I had a sudden strong urge to stop and go back to the car. I turned around and looked, couldn't figure out why I should go back to the car, and shrugged off the impression. Discovering that the gate was indeed locked, and mentally kicking myself for such a waste of time, I turned to see the car, having slipped out of gear, traveling in reverse making a wide circle in the street.

Screaming and hollering, I ran after the car trying to catch up to the open door. If I wasn't in such a panic I might have had the sense to run in the opposite direction and hop in when the open door came around. As it was, I began running alongside of it. Each time around brought the metal monster closer to the house across the street. The thought of my car careening into the neighbor's living room and having them come home from work to find their home collapsed into a neat little pile of firewood was enough to curl my hair (on my head, not my toes). The splintering sound of wood snapping as the car backed over the mailbox post, along with my frantic shrieks for help, alerted the man next door that something had gone awry. Leaping over a hedge in a magnificent display of heroism, he raced to the car, nearly breaking his leg as he managed to stumble in and stop the possessed vehicle just as it was making a final mad dash for the garage.

Two things resulted from that little exercise to hear the Still Small Voice; first, I had to replace the mailbox. Second, I wasn't any closer to recognizing the still, small voice than I was before, except that what I thought was the Spirit *wasn't*, and what I didn't think was the Spirit *was*. It was so confusing to me. I knew I would have to find the right kind of exercise to practice hearing the Spirit. The opportunity was soon to come.

A friend from BFA (Benjamin Franklin Academy, where I was an administrator for a semester) told me that Max Skousen was coming to town to do a little in-home seminar on deepening our spiritual walk. Max was the brother of prolific LDS author and lecturer Cleon Skousen. Max gave a fireside[2] at someone's house a few weeks before in which he talked about the subconscious mind and how we can harness its healing power through an exercise he called "RFA" (Relaxed Focused Attention). He said that the Tree of Knowledge of Good and Evil was given to humanity in the Garden of Eden to break our hearts; to make us realize that we *can't* do it all, so we could come to the Lord and surrender.

I felt ready at that point to let Heavenly Father work in my life in a way I hadn't let him before. Listening to Max that evening gave me hope. It was different from the usual things we were taught at church, like doing everything we possibly could first, and then God would help us. Wasn't it somewhere in the Bible that "God helps those who help themselves?" (It's not). And yet I felt helpless to help myself. I couldn't wait until Max came back to give his weekend-long seminar. The fireside had just been a teaser.

The first night of the seminar Max pointed out aspects of the gospel we hadn't heard before in church. For example, he quoted D & C 59:21, which says, "And in nothing doth man offend God, or against none is his wrath kindled, save those who confess not his hand in all things, and obey not his commandments." Then Max explained that we should be thankful for *all* things, including black widow spiders, rattlesnakes, and Hitler; not that we should condone what Hitler and other tyrants did, but that we should be thankful that they played their roles in providing opposition to the heaven we once lived in. I really didn't feel right about what he was saying, but it was certainly an interesting perspective.

After the lecture we were told to split off into pairs to do exercises with each other. Before I had a chance to pair up with someone I knew and trusted, a guy I didn't want to do an RFA with picked me as a partner. I felt really uncomfortable divulging possibly my deepest secrets, that even I didn't know existed, in such a public manner. What if I regressed in my memories back to my mother's womb or to the preexistence? It would be like undressing in front of strangers. I asked my friend, Alaine, to demonstrate RFAs with the guy while I watched (sounds kinky) and fortunately the time ran out before I had to do it.

The next activity was an exercise called "connected breathing," and everyone was having some wonderful experience except me. Some people were seeing visions, while others were getting incredible feelings. My eyes welled up with tears as I silently prayed, asking Heavenly Father what was wrong with me. Was I not worthy enough? Did I not have enough faith? Or perhaps what they were all doing was wrong and the Lord was protecting me.

The longer the deep breathing exercises went on, the stranger the phenomena exhibited by participants. Some of the people lying on the floor began laughing hysterically. Other people were sobbing uncontrollably. The ones not laughing or crying were moaning and sighing. So, I did what any sane person would do; I got up, went into the kitchen, filled a plate with yummy snacks, and sat down to watch the show.

After things calmed down and all the participants' emotions were spent, we gathered in the living room to share our experiences. When it was my turn I said

I felt like an outsider looking in. I felt like a wanderer on a cold winter night who finds a large cottage. The door is locked. I look in the window and see smiling people warming themselves by a cheery fire, obviously enjoying themselves. All I can do is watch from the outside, alone and powerless, while everyone else is having the time of their lives.

Sunday evening was the last night of the workshop. Scott came with me. Max demonstrated a procedure called "muscle testing." He asked Scott to come up and hold his arm out and try to resist when Max pressed down. Scott easily resisted. Then Max had Scott hold a cup of sugar, which he explained is bad for the body and that it would sap strength from Scott. Then Max pushed on Scott's arm and Scott still resisted. So Max pushed down harder, but Scott was still able to hold his arm out. Max looked a little chagrined. He told Scott to sit down, and explained how unusual it was for muscle-testing not to work. Scott was skeptical the whole time. He figured if it was a real scientific principle it wouldn't be so subjective.

Max's weekend workshop ended in disappointment for me. When I told Pat about it at my singing lesson, she said that muscle-testing was of the devil and should be avoided. She suggested that maybe the reason I felt like an outsider looking in was that Heavenly Father had protected me from being deceived. If that was the case I was truly grateful; but Brother Skousen's odd ideas aside, I seemed to get the short end of the stick when it came to the Spirit handing out promptings, dreams, visions, and spiritual experiences.

No matter, I purposed in my heart to continue being faithful, magnify my church callings,[3] and strive to live worthy of the blessings of the gospel.

---

1. *Teachings of the Presidents of the Church: Brigham Young.* (The Church of Jesus Christ of Latter-day Saints. Salt Lake City, UT, 1997) 16-17
2. A "fireside" in the LDS context is a meeting usually held on a Sunday evening (but not always), in which there is a guest speaker, followed by fellowship and refreshments.
3. In LDS vernacular, to magnify one's callings means to enlarge or develop them; to give your best efforts.

CHAPTER 16

Had My Cake and Wore it Too

Fate, it seems, is not without a sense of irony.

—Morpheus , The Matrix

She ran out of Relief Society swearing, yelling, and crying, with a couple ladies trailing after her to calm her down. I hadn't planned on the lesson going so badly. It was supposed to be a great Relief Society lesson. I planned so carefully to make this one stand out. I always began with humor, a gripping analogy, or a demonstration of some sort to make a point and drive the message home. This time was no different at first. The topic was reverence. The message I wanted to convey was that the gospel is a beautiful thing and must be handled with care. It was very important to treat it with reverence and respect.

To illustrate my point, I bought a beautifully decorated angel food cake topped with whipped cream and strawberries. I set the cake, which rested on a crystal pedestal serving plate, on the table next to the podium. I began by saying I brought a cake to share with everyone, but that it was too delicious to wait till the end of class, so I asked who wanted a piece right away. Several of the ladies raised their hands.

With a smile on my face, I drove my hand directly into the cake, grasped a handful of it, and slapped it onto a paper plate, scraping as much as possible off my fingers. I then looked for the closest person to the front who had their hand raised—Sister Bates—and handed it to her.

Now, Sister Bates was probably in her sixties. She was a fairly new member of the Church and the only black person in our ward. She was probably the only black person in the whole stake. In fact, she was probably the only black Mormon in North Las Vegas at the time. Well, the whole class broke out into laughter from the shock and surprise of me using my hand instead of a serving knife to dish out the cake. That is, everyone except Sister Bates, who just kind of sat there with a stunned look on her face. I guess she hadn't sat in on very many of my lessons before.

After the laughter died down I went on to explain the "object lesson," saying that the cake represented the gospel of Jesus Christ and how we should have reverence for it. Just as we wouldn't want to serve a beautiful cake in such a crass manner, we shouldn't take the gospel lightly or treat it irreverently.

A few minutes later Sister Bates stood up abruptly and walked up the aisle toward me with the plate of cake in her shaking hands. I didn't know if she, A) was going to set it down on the table; B) ask for a second helping, or; C) wanted to give me a hug for such a brilliant analogy. The answer was "D) none of the above." Instead, she drew back her hand and slammed the cake into the side of my face, screamed, and ran out of the room swearing. I'll bet it was the only time such language had ever been used in our building. I was just thankful I gave her the cake on a paper plate and not one made from cast iron. I quickly called after her, "I'm sorry," although I didn't know exactly what I was apologizing for.

Immediately after all the gasps sucked the air from the room, it became as quiet as a tomb. Even nursing babes in arms stopped cooing and suckling as the tension built. I was dumbfounded and didn't know what to think. My first thought was that Sister Bates felt I was being irreverent in the Lord's House, but that was kind of an overreaction, in my opinion. My mind was racing, and I knew I could easily burst into tears if I didn't get my emotions quickly under control. The part of me that was a professional singer and entertainer said *The Show Must Go On.* The sisters had come to church to be fed, and I intended to feed them (no pun intended) (actually the pun *was* intended).

So I did what any self-respecting teacher would do; wiping a strawberry slice from my eye and whipped cream from my nose and right ear, I went on with the lesson. My demeanor may have appeared calm, but my legs were shaking. The Relief Society president came up in tears and gave me a quick hug, while one of the ladies took a napkin and began removing cake from my hair. I felt like a baboon being picked over by another primate, but with all the decorum I could muster, I delivered the rest of my message with Sister McCormick preening me. I don't even remember what all I said because my mouth was saying one thing while my brain was thinking something else. *Had I been irreverent? Was anyone else besides Sister Bates offended? If I ever became rich and famous could I get someone to primp my hair for me on a regular basis?*

After class was over, several of the women came up and hugged me, offering words of encouragement and support. I gathered my things and stepped out into the hall just as Scott came up with a concerned look on his face.

"Are you okay? Did something happen? The bishop told me I needed to find you right away to comfort you." He looked me over, trying to survey the damage, if any. "What happened to your hair?"

"I'm fine. Sister Bates smashed cake in my face, not sure why, but I'll survive. That was *some cake*."

"That must have been *some lesson*," Scott remarked as we went to get the kids out of their classes.

"One of my best," I smiled.

By Sunday afternoon I had my answer. Sister Bates had thought I purposely handed her the cake in a disrespectful way because she was black. All day I was still in the disbelief stage. By Monday I was mad. Tuesday I was really mad. How dare she assume that just because I'm white I have disdain for black people? I was offended by her racism. But then I tried to analyze it and see things from her perspective. She was a senior citizen and had probably lived through a lot of the racism that existed prior to the 1970's. She most likely experienced having to sit at the back of the bus or drink from a different water fountain than white people at one time in her life.

My heart began to soften toward her. I bought her a rose and a card on which I wrote an apology for offending her. I said I had respect for her and by no means meant to hurt her feelings, and that I gave her the cake only because she was clos-est to the front of the room. I wrote that I hoped she would come back to church and that there was no need for her to be embarrassed or uncomfortable, because we all valued her friendship and wanted her there.

I got quite a shiner from the impact, but by the next Sunday my right eye and cheek had turned from black and purple to yellow and green as the blood cells broke down into bilirubin. The whole week after the incident, I received tons of cards and goodies from different ward members. Two weeks later Sister Bates returned to church. I walked into Relief Society and immediately saw her sitting on the end of the second row. Although my first thought was to avoid her like the plague because I still felt hurt, I went up to her, smiled, and said,

"Sister Bates, what a beautiful blue dress you have on today! It looks so flattering on you."

She straightened herself in her chair, adjusted her hat (she was the only one to wear a hat to church), smiled and replied, "Thank you."

I was glad I had done the right thing. There was no tension between us from then on. It seemed like after the incident and the way I handled it, my popularity in the ward soared. People looked at me a little differently. Instead of feeling like a misfit, I felt like a hero.

A few months later, sometime in late September or early October, our Relief Society president, Sister Walker, passed away from a severe asthma attack. She was a diminutive lady, wheelchair bound when her seasonal allergies got so bad she didn't have the strength to walk. She was rather quiet, but a woman of character and conviction. The bishop told me he really had no clue what Relief Society was all about until Sister Walker taught him through her example of serving others. She knew exactly what was needed and frequently put her foot down with the bishop, telling him what to do and how, in regard to the women of the Relief Society. I'm thankful she paved the way, because it wasn't too long after her passing that I began to notice the bishop looking at me a little differently too.

I started getting a very uneasy feeling every time I went to church and saw Bishop Herdt glancing at me. I wished he would hurry up and call somebody to be the new R.S. president because I was afraid he might be contemplating calling me! Maybe I was being paranoid; after all, I was hardly Relief Society president material. I guess all I could do was prepare for the possibility while staying focused on pursuing my dreams. Regardless of what would come about, it was time to buckle in for the ride.

My plan was twofold; first, to become an Education Week speaker to encourage and edify the Saints; and second, to write books and sing within the Christian community to bring people into the Mormon Church. I had no desire to run the Relief Society; I had bigger fish to fry. I didn't know it at the time, but a "bigger fish" would be instrumental in frying *me*.

CHAPTER 17

From Frumpy to Fabulous
(with a little help from Oprah)

...buckle up, Dorothy, 'cause Kansas is going bye-bye.

—Cypher, The Matrix

My 11-year-old son, Curran, worked hard all summer for the neighborhood ice cream man to buy an expensive, but ugly fish (actually it *was* butt-ugly); a Jack Dempsey. He had the fish for about two weeks when we decided to go to the park as a family. We were gone for a couple of hours. Upon our return, Curran declared that the fish was gone. A diligent fish-hunt ensued, and the Dempsey was found floundering on the windowsill. The poor thing had taken a swimming leap to capture its goldfish dinner, but with no lid to stop him, sailed right out of the tank. Amazingly, it was still alive; though barely. I knew my son was heart-broken. He came to me in tears, asking what he should do. I recommended putting the fish back into the tank to see if it would revive. The Dempsey sunk to the bottom and laid there, its sides heaving with every "breath." I wanted to tell Curran to pray for the life of his fish, but I was afraid that if Heavenly Father let it die, it would shake his faith in prayer and in the Lord.

Have you ever felt like your prayers were bouncing off the ceiling? So often I had gone to Heavenly Father in prayer asking for answers to problems. I followed what D&C 9:8-9 said about making a decision, presenting it to God, and then waiting for a burning in the bosom or a "stupor of thought." I often had a stupor of thought, but the only time I seemed to get a "burning in the bosom" was when leaning over a hot stove. I tried everything to "hear" the answers, but they rarely seemed to come.

Maybe this time it would be different. Maybe this time, for the sake of my little boy, Heavenly Father would answer my prayers. Seeking privacy, I shut the door to my room, knelt at my bedside, and wept before Heavenly Father in behalf of the Dempsey. "Please," I prayed, "please heal the fish miraculously so that Curran's faith in Thee will be strengthened and his testimony of the gospel will grow. But if not, then please make it die quickly so it doesn't have to suffer."

I checked on my son and his fish. Curran had propped the Dempsey up against an undulating plastic pirate ship that gave the aquarium a nice, homey feel for its residents. It seemed the fish might actually recuperate.

The next day brought no change in the Dempsey's condition. As a matter of fact, there was no change at all in the ensuing days, other than the wretched creature would sometimes flop over and have to be propped back up. Daily I prayed for that fish, anticipating the great miracle Heavenly Father was going to perform. It would be a defining moment in our lives, something Curran would reflect on when he grew up and was a General Authority giving a talk in General Conference;

"Yes, brothers and sisters," I imagined him testifying at the grand pulpit, "I knew there was a God in Heaven the day He healed my fish. That was the moment I determined to serve the Lord for the rest of my life. That was the moment I gained a testimony of the Church of Jesus Christ of Latter-day Saints, blah, blah, blah."

And I would beam proudly from the front row, nudging the Saint sitting next to me, "That's my boy up there. The Miracle of the Fish happened over 30 years ago and look at what my son has become. Yes, that's my boy."

Secretly I harbored the thought, "If the fish revives, then I will absolutely *know* that the Church is true." Sadly, the fish lingered in that nether-land between life and death for almost two weeks. The heavens were like brass. I became discouraged. What kind of pleasure did God take in the suffering of this fish? Didn't He love us enough? Pinning my spiritual hopes on a fish might seem a bit silly, but I frequently heard or read of other miracles in Mormon talks and literature.

One Education Week speaker told about a dehydrated pet frog that miraculously regenerated after being prayed over by a child. Apparently the lad found a frog by a pond, put it in his pocket, and promptly forgot about it. He found the dried up amphibian days later, and with childlike faith in prayer, went to the Lord asking that the frog would "wake up." The dead frog twitched, and a moment later hopped out of the boy's hand. Were we so unworthy as to not merit this one favor? Was my child's testimony of the Church not as important as the boy's whose frog re-inflated?

Finally the day came that we either had to flush, bury, or barbeque the Dempsey. We buried it. I was still mad at the Lord and glad I hadn't encouraged Curran to pray for the fish. It was about this time that I was called to be the Relief Society president. During the time of the Dempsey drama, I was eagerly awaiting a call from the Oprah Winfrey Show, telling me that I was one of the chosen few who would be getting a "Millennial Make-Over." I'd already sent pictures of myself to the studio, and the days were crawling by. I didn't watch much TV, and all I knew about Oprah was that she was a celebrity with a daily show. Someone either told me or I read a short article about Oprah looking for guests on her program, so I had gone to her website and looked at upcoming shows that might be of interest.

The phone rang as I was heading out the door for a class. I wouldn't have answered it at all had it not been for my hope of quasi-stardom. It was the bishop.

"Sister Crookston," he greeted, "do you know what the Relief Society Emblem is?"

I'd been teaching R.S. lessons for six years, but I really hadn't the foggiest notion.

"Two stalks of wheat," he answered. He then asked if I knew what the Relief Society flower was. Frankly I didn't know there was a Relief Society flower. Apparently it's the sego lily. I think a better flower would be the *busy lizzie* (impatiens). I wondered if the priesthood had a flower too. Hmmm...maybe the *narcissus*? He asked if I knew the Relief Society colors. I'm sure he thought I must be a complete dunderhead. I took a wild guess, reasoning that the Cub Scout colors were blue and gold, so maybe there was a connection. I got the answer right. His next question was regarding the motto of the Relief Society. I was uncertain, but supposed it had something to do with charity.

"Yes. *Charity never faileth*," he replied.

"Really," I said, afraid of where the conversation was heading. "Well, I've learned something new today."

The bishop then asked me about my philosophy on home schooling—probably trying to ascertain whether I was some sort of activist (I wasn't)—and what I thought about Joseph Smith and Brigham Young. He asked about my family. The minutes were ticking by. I was getting antsy to get to my class, as it was the last one for the semester and the teacher was bringing Krispy Crème doughnuts. I told the bishop that I hated to cut short the scintillating conversation, but I was going to be late to the college. I hung up the phone, speculating that he was considering me for a new calling.

Driving to class I sat a little straighter. On campus I walked a little taller, and began to feel somewhat "presidential." If people were going to begin looking to me as a leader, I had better start acting "leaderly." It was hard to look leaderly though, in holey jeans (before it was fashionable), a toddler-stained tee shirt, and my uncombed hair in a ponytail. The morning had been so hectic I'd forgotten to properly groom myself. How embarrassing (or how A.D.D.).

The following day I checked Oprah's website, and saw that they already had the guests lined up for the make-over show. I was really disappointed, but deluded myself into believing it was a sign that I would not be called as the next Relief Society president, which brought me some comfort. I reasoned that if my greatest dream wasn't going to come true, neither would my worst nightmare. It appeared I wasn't good enough to be on Oprah, and probably wasn't good enough to be a leader in the Church. In the end, I was wrong on both accounts.

Three days later the bishop called from Utah where he was vacationing with his family. He asked if I would serve in the capacity of Relief Society president.

"Would it surprise you if I said I knew you would call me for the last three weeks?" I asked. He said it wouldn't.

Of course I accepted; that's what good church members do. A calling from the Bishop is a calling from God himself. The bishop later confessed to me that he had reservations, but the Spirit made it clear to him that if he did not call me to be the next R.S. president he would be under condemnation. The bishop advised me to start thinking of who I would like as my two counselors. Actually, I'd already been thinking about it.

I truly felt like a fish out of water. My only hope was that Heavenly Father would not let me flounder like the Dempsey. I chose two counselors who were almost as untraditional as I was. We all home schooled, we all believed the Second Coming of Jesus Christ was near, and we all felt that the sisters needed more focus in their lives on the simple things. Trying to juggle husbands, kids, callings, and everything else, we often joked among ourselves that we must have been the most dysfunctional Relief Society presidency that the ward had ever had.

A few months later, in February of 2000, I again attempted to get on the Oprah Winfrey Show. The theme was changing your frumpy clothing wardrobe into something more stylish. Well, I could do frumpy; that was right up my alley. I had my daughter video tape me singing "The Frumpy Clothes Blues." I changed the words to the old standard "Ballin' the Jack;"

> I wake up every mornin', put a tee-shirt on,
> Slip into my sweats that are baggy and long,
> White, cushy socks and athletic shoes,
> That's why I'm singin' the frumpy clothes blues.
> I slick my hair back into a pony tail,
> Don a little blush so I don't look so pale.
> But I don't want to look like this anymore;
> I want to look great when I go to the store.
> The frumpy clothes blues...

It was just hokey enough that two days after sending the tape by overnight mail, someone on Oprah's staff called me to ask if I would like to visit Chicago.

On February 7, 2000, at 5:45 in the morning, Quinn drove me to the airport to catch a plane to the Windy City. It was an exciting flight. They served little omelets and biscuits for breakfast (yum). But the most exciting part of the flight was when I reached into my backpack to pull out a mini-cassette recorder and accidently pulled out the pin on a personal alarm I had tucked away.

All of a sudden there was a piercing *wat wat wat* type of wail blasting from my backpack and reverberating throughout the cabin. My heart immediately leapt to my throat as I frantically began digging around for the unit from which the cord and pin had separated. Concerned and frightened passengers were turning their heads in confusion as the flight attendant rushed down the aisle toward me, eyes bulging (okay, maybe not bulging, but popping out just a little bit) demanding, "What is that? *What is that?*"

I explained that I inadvertently pulled the pin out of my personal alarm *unintentionally*. She hovered over me as I continued to grope through my over-packed carry-on until I finally located the device. I was so flustered and embarrassed, and my hands were shaking so badly, I couldn't get the pin into the hole to shut the stupid thing off. Finally, after what seemed like an eternity, pin and hole united, and sweet silence prevailed. Almost immediately a voice came over the intercom announcing there was no cause for alarm (ha!); that it was just some idiot's portable car alarm blaring. Well, at least that's what *I* would have said. But really, the attendant told everyone to stay calm; that someone's beeper just went off and everything was under control.

Well, after that fiasco, I didn't dare look for the cassette recorder again, so I just kind of slunk down in my seat and very carefully removed a Church *Ensign* magazine from a side-pocket of my backpack to read for a bit before we landed and—as I could only imagination—they carted me off the plane in a strait-jacket or shackles. Fortunately, I was able to freely exit the plane without creating any further disturbance. A woman standing near the gate held a sign with "CROOKSTON" written in big, bold letters. She walked me out to the curb where a limousine was waiting. It was quite an experience. Imagine a poor, jean-and-t-shirt--clad, "frumpy" mother of nine being transported by limo to a Five Star hotel and treated to dining at one of Chicago's finest restaurants.

As I sat by myself at a table among finely dressed, upper class patrons, I had to attempt to act dainty while eating instead of shoveling the food in my mouth as I normally did. You see, there are only two kinds of people in large families; the quick and the hungry; therefore, "dainty" wasn't ever an option. Even while trying to eat carefully, my bosom still ended up looking like a snack tray. I discreetly brushed away crumbs, chunks, and heaven knows what else onto the floor before someone walking by thought I was offering hors d'oeuvres.

The trip was a dream-come-true: Harried Housewife transformed into Glamour Girl (that's *h-a-r-r-i-e-d*, folks, not *hairy*. I actually shaved my legs for the occasion). The next morning I was taken to Harpo Studios where the Frumpy Clothes Makeover segment was to be filmed in front of a live audience. There were two of us who were actual housewives, while the other four or five women were professional models. We were primped, powdered, coiffed, clothed, and coached on how to enter the stage and model our outfits. One of the directors told me he wanted me to kind of jog down the ramp onto the stage with my hands in the air and give a energetic "woo hoo!" Then I was to turn and spin in my trendy outfit while encouraging the audience to applaud. That wasn't going to happen. I was really self-conscious, being almost fifty pounds overweight and suddenly gripped with stage fright.

Somehow I was able to walk onto the stage and smile (both at the same time) without tripping or otherwise embarrassing myself or Oprah. They had a recording of my song playing in the background. That was pretty cool. As soon as I made my exit from the stage, I was whisked into a room and told to carefully hang the clothes up so they could be returned to the department store that loaned them to the show. I was surprised and disappointed. I thought I was getting a whole new wardrobe to take home. I arrived frumpy and was leaving grumpy.

I reluctantly put my t-shirt back on, slipped into my sweats that were baggy and long, donned my men's socks and tattered athletic shoes, and was about to leave Harpo singing the Frumpy Clothes Blues. As I slowly walked toward the exit, Oprah came hurrying down the corridor toward some unknown destination with a string of people trailing her.

Looking somewhat surprised, she stopped and asked me, "Why aren't you wearing your new outfit?"

"They told me the clothes were on loan and I had to give them back."

"That's wrong. That's just plain wrong." Oprah declared. "Mary!" She snapped her fingers. "Mary! See that this woman gets those clothes back. I don't have time to deal with this now." She turned to me once more and said, "I'm really very sorry. We'll see that you're taken care of," and with that she turned on her heels and continued on her way. I thought that was so gracious of her. While I don't share her views on many issues, I must say she is a very impressive, big-hearted woman.

One of the models who appeared on the show was kind enough to invite me to stay the night at her apartment before I flew back to Las Vegas. All I remember about her was her name; Sarah. She and her husband were born-again Christians. I wasn't sure what that meant exactly, other than my previous exposure to so-called born-again Christians was not very pleasant. This couple, however, was different. There was something about them that was winsome and appealing.

In the morning they fed me a hearty breakfast, and the husband asked if he could talk to me about God. Of course I said yes. This was a "missionary opportunity" for me to tell him about the LDS Church. He was very respectful as he asked me about the Mormon view of God, Jesus, and the Holy Spirit. He couldn't grasp the idea that each person in the Godhead was a separate, distinct, individual god. They were "one in purpose, not form," I explained.

With mild frustration I asked, "What difference does it make *what* a person thinks about God? Does it really matter whether he is a physical being or a big puff-ball in the sky? God is God is God, regardless of what anyone thinks he is made of, right?"

"It matters," he said, as he showed me Scripture verses from the Bible, but I just couldn't see his point. It didn't make any sense to me.

I thanked the couple for their hospitality and left to explore Chicago for the day before catching my flight home.

CHAPTER 18

Return of the Other Woman

I imagine that right now, you're feeling a bit like Alice, hmm? Tumbling down the rabbit hole?
—Morpheus , The Matrix

God works in mysterious ways. The evening the show aired (February 11, 2000), I got a surprising phone call from an unforgettable person; Becky Talley—my mortal enemy from the past; the "other woman" from the love triangle 20 years before. I still didn't like her very much, even though all was forgiven (seeing how I won). To me she was still "Pinhead," the affectionate appellation I had once given her due to the fact that my motorcycle helmet (which was a men's size small) was too big for her back when Scott picked us up for dates on his motorcycle. She couldn't wear the spare helmet Scott had because it was too large, so Scott would always borrow mine for Becky to use on their dates. Sheesh! Why couldn't she buy her own helmet instead of getting cooties on mine?

Becky had lost track of us over the years; however, on the day the Frumpy Clothes Makeover show aired, her boss sent her home early (Divine coincidence?). She turned on the TV and hit the VCR record button, which she later told me was something she normally didn't do. She hardly ever watched television, let alone Oprah. Becky sat down a while later to watch the tape. Within a minute of playback I came out onto the stage. Becky took a double take.

"*Could that really be Tracy?*" she wondered. Of course I looked the same drop-dead gorgeous after 20 years. Of course she recognized me. The guest wardrobe designer mentioned my first name, number of children, and the city I lived in. Becky took the opportunity to look me up and call.

We had a pleasant conversation, although I was shocked to learn that Becky left the Church only a few months before. She was a several generation Latter-day Saint from pioneer stock and as True Blue as they came; no R-rated movies or caffeinated sodas, an expert in baking, cooking, canning, sewing, underwater basket-weaving with her toes (not really; but she could have), and hanging on every word of every General Conference talk. She was a straight arrow if ever there was one.

Becky explained that she had been diligently reading and studying the Bible and eventually it led her out of Mormonism. My first thought was that the Lord arranged everything so I could bring her back into the Church. I made a commitment to read the Bible myself to see what could possibly be in there that would lead her astray.

Over the following months we kept up a correspondence, and Becky would always tell me about what the Lord was doing in her life. She kept expressing that she had never felt as close to the Savior as she did now, and that the "truth had set her free." It certainly puzzled me as to why Heavenly Father would lead her out of His "True Church." Not only that, but apostates were supposed to lose the Spirit completely and become dark, bitter, empty individuals. In fact, Brigham Young said that the skin of apostates turns black.[1] Instead, quite the opposite had happened; Becky was calm, peaceful, and had an assurance about her standing with God. Additionally, she was just as white as ever, wrinkle-free, and minimally gray. I kept looking for a chink in her new armor; evidence that she was being led astray by the devil, but could find none.

As the summer wore on I began to pray to know the truth. Not that I doubted the truthfulness of the Church; I just wanted know how it could be that Becky and others could have a close relationship with the Lord *outside* of the Church, especially as "apostates." Could it be that there was more than one way to the Celestial Kingdom?

On one of our evening walks, my husband posed an intriguing question. He asked, "If the Church isn't true, would you want to know?" After pondering for a moment, I responded that I would not want to know. If the Church wasn't true, then what *was*? If the Church wasn't true, the very foundation of the world as we knew it—our lifestyle, belief system, and way of thinking—would crumble. The mere thought of it was too scary to contemplate.

In August, the kids and I drove up to Provo for BYU Education Week. It was just as uplifting as ever. My high school friend, Brad Wilcox, taught several classes at the event. Since graduating, he had become an author and popular Church Education System speaker, in addition to teaching elementary school students. I asked him how I could become an Education Week speaker, and if he would give me a favorable recommendation. He said he would be happy to. I always wanted to become an Education Week speaker so I could make a difference in the lives of fellow Saints. I hoped Brad could help me get my foot in the door.

While we were in Provo, my sister-in-law Sherry told me about a woman named Gail Smith who had some dreams about the End Times and claimed her deceased sister had visited her from the spirit world. She was interviewed on a few local radio programs, and was later warned by church leaders to stop speaking publicly or face church discipline. She ended up getting excommunicated. Sherry arranged for us to meet with her. We spent most of the afternoon listening to Gail's story. She seemed really sincere. Although I didn't agree with her review of the Church and its leaders, I believed she really had some supernatural experiences.

Now I was more mystified than ever. How could someone who had been excommunicated get visions and visitations from the dead; someone else who left the Church on her own, experience the peace that passes all understanding; and faithful members all be getting a spiritual witness that the course they were on was the "true" course? I was discovering that people of many different religions have spiritual experiences, so experiences couldn't be the basis for finding truth. I decided I had to know the truth at all costs.

I fervently prayed that Heavenly Father would reveal the truth to me. I told him that if the Church really was true, I wanted to know *beyond* any shadow of doubt so that I could continue to press forward in faith in preparation for the Second Coming; and if it was not true, then I needed to know that too. I felt an urgency to be on the correct side when Jesus came again. When I prayed I wouldn't be deceived, I never considered the possibility that I already *had* been deceived by the very institution I considered infallible.

God took me at my word that I really desired truth and began leading me into finding it. A few weeks later I remembered Sherry had once told me about a paper she came across that *if it were true*, she said, was the scariest thing she had ever read. She said she was reluctant to send it to me because she didn't want to be responsible for "shaking my testimony." She would only say that it was about the temple ceremony. I assured her that I had my free agency (free will) and that I absolved her from all blame. If what was written was true, I needed to know. If it were *not* true, then the Lord would give me discernment.

A few days before October General Conference, the anticipated paper arrived. It was about seven or eight pages long, written by some guy from Southern Utah. He quoted Book of Mormon witness David Whitmer saying that Joseph Smith was a fallen prophet. He also made references to the temple ceremony being copied from Masonic Temple rites. The information was mildly interesting to me, but for the most part I dismissed it as the exaggerated ranting of a very deceived individual. What *did* grab my attention though, were some alleged quotes by Brigham Young concerning blood atonement.

According to the writer, Young said;

> Suppose you found your brother in bed with your wife, and put a javelin through the both of them, you would be justified and they would atone for their sins, and be received into the kingdom of God. I would at once do so in such a case; and under such circumstances, I have no wife whom I love so well that I would not put a javelin through her heart, and I would do so with clean hands...[2]

Young allegedly went on to say that "the blood of Christ will never wipe that out [adultery], your own blood must atone for it." I was skeptical and incredulous. This was obviously misquoted or taken out of context.

Up until this point as a Mormon, I never verified quotes or teachings of the Church when someone made reference to them. I took the person's word for it. It never dawned on me that the person telling me might, A) have an agenda, or B) be mistaken. This time I decided to see for myself.

Right away I began calling people in my ward to see if anyone had the Journal of Discourses in their personal library. The first five or six people I called didn't own a set. Someone suggested I call Brother Bennion, as he had quite a collection of books. Success. I jumped into my van and headed for his house. I had a list of references written down from the article my sister-in-law sent me, and began going through the volumes. To my astonishment I found that the quotes were genuine and not taken out of context. I looked up several topics that had disturbed me; the Adam-God theory, blacks being denied the priesthood, monogamy condemned, and blood atonement.

I found many outrageous doctrines before leaving Brother Bennion's house. As I was leaving, he asked me if I found what I was looking for. I replied I found a whole lot more than I was looking for. I gave him the example of the Adam-God doctrine.[3] Brother Bennion defended Brigham Young by saying he had only speculated on it publicly a few times, which I later found wasn't so. It was neither speculation, nor an obscure teaching.

When I joined the Church in the 1970's, members were encouraged to purchase the Journal of Discourses to use for family study. Now I was being told that the Journal of Discourses was unreliable. I wondered how they could be unreliable when they are transcripts of the talks and teachings of the prophets and apostles of the Church. Furthermore, current prophets and apostles often quoted from the Journal of Discourses in their own writings and conference addresses. It seemed to me there was a double standard. The Journal of Discourses had First Presidency approval at the time of publication[4] and for over a century since. All the sermons had been printed in the Church newspaper prior to being published in book form.

I went home quite shaken. Many of the things President Young taught conflicted with my understanding of the gospel. For example, the teaching that the blood of Christ doesn't atone for all sins was contrary to the account in the gospel of John, chapter 8, verses 8-11, in which a woman caught in the very act of adultery was taken before Jesus to see what he would say. With compassion he told the woman he did not condemn her, but that she should go her way and sin no more. He didn't say anything about javelins or paying for her sin with her own blood. I would have to do some research to learn more.

---

1. Concerning faithful members of the Church, Young said, "You can see men and women who are sixty or seventy years of age looking young and handsome; but let them apostatize and they will become gray-haired, wrinkled, and black, just like the devil." (Journal of Discourses, Vol. 5, p. 332)
2. Journal of Discourses, volume 3, p. 247
3. Brigham Young, as well as members of the Twelve, taught for over 25 years that Adam is our God and the father of our spirits. The Church no longer teaches that doctrine; however, to deny it was ever taught or considered to be true is misleading.
4. *Journal of Discourses, Vol. 1* p. A LETTER FROM THE FIRST PRESIDENCY. June 1, 1853. "Dear Brethren – It is well known to many of you, that Elder George D. Watt, by our counsel, spent much time in the midst of poverty and hardships to acquire the art of reporting in Phonography, which he has faithfully and fully accomplished; and he has been reporting the public Sermons, Discourses, Lectures, &c., Delivered by the Presidency, the Twelve, and others in this city, for nearly two years, almost without fee or reward. Elder Watt now proposes to publish a Journal of these reports, in England, for the benefit of the Saints at large, and to obtain means to enable him to sustain his highly useful position of Reporter. You will perceive at once that this will be a work of mutual benefit, and we cheerfully and warmly request your cooperation in the purchase and sale of the

above-named Journal, and wish all the profits arising therefrom to be under the control of Elder Watt" (signed; Brigham Young, Heber C. Kimball, Willard Richards)

CHAPTER 19

The Truth unfolds

I can't explain everything to you. I'm sure that it's all going to seem very strange...
—Trinity , The Matrix

I called Becky to ask her about the website she recommended months before. It was a web address that I blew off because I "already had the truth, so why look?" Now I was very interested in seeing what www.hismin.com had to offer. Along with researching on the Internet, I checked out some books from the library; *Mormon America* by Richard and Joan Ostling, *In Sacred Loneliness* by Todd Compton (LDS author and researcher), and *Mormon Hierarchy: Origins of Power* by Michael D. Quinn (former BYU history professor; now an independent scholar).

Scott and I read voraciously for weeks, checking every reference we could with Church records, histories, and official publications to verify the many contradictions, inconsistencies, and revisions in Mormon history. We didn't want to take anyone's word for anything; we wanted to see for ourselves. All the while I prayed fervently that God would guide me and not let me be led astray. I only wanted to know the truth.

Becky kept telling me the god of Mormonism was not the same as God in the Bible. I didn't exactly understand that concept, but didn't want to take any chances; so I began addressing my prayers to "the God of Abraham, Isaac, and Jacob." If the

Church was true, my prayers would still reach Heavenly Father, but if it wasn't true, the real God would hear and respond to my pleas.

I emailed several ex-Mormon websites asking for answers to my many questions, and references I could look up. I sent away for pamphlets and whatever reading material was available. We visited with LDS Institute teachers and relatives active in the Church whose opinions we respected. We stayed up till two and three in the morning—night after night, week after week—reading, researching, studying, and praying that the truth would make itself known.

When I read for myself the almost word for word similarities between the temple endowment blood oaths[1] and the oaths taken in Masonic rituals, I removed my temple garments. I reasoned that if I was wrong, the Lord would forgive me because my intentions were pure; I'd been praying and fasting, and only wanted the truth. However, if I was right, *perhaps the garments were actually shielding me from receiving the truth.*

My 15-year-old daughter was the first one to notice I wasn't wearing my garments any more. News quickly spread throughout the household. Understandably, all the older children were upset, which only added to the turmoil I was already going through. I wrote in my journal:

October 29, 2000:

I found pictures of occult symbols on the [Salt Lake] temple and read and compared Masonic ceremonies to the Mormon temple ceremonies. They were almost identical. It really bothers me that the LDS Church discourages the use of the cross as a symbol, yet have the pentagram—a recognized satanic symbol—on a holy edifice. And the explanations by the Church seemed pretty lame to me, especially if we are supposed to avoid even the appearance of evil. I've been so upset! For two weeks I was tormented by the thought and wonder of whether God really exists, and if he knows and loves me personally. The rug was pulled out from under me. For 26 years my only frame of reference has been the Mormon gospel. If Mormonism isn't true, then what *is*? Is there *any* truth out there? A purpose? A plan? It's scary; real scary! Anyway, I've been vacillating back and forth between believing the Church is true and that the Church isn't true. But, the more I learn and study, the more I realize I was deceived. In the Church I know who I am, who I was, who I will become. My patriarchal blessing tells me of the great and valiant spirit I was in the pre-existence, the wonderful mission and things I will accomplish in this life, and a little about my life after the resurrection. According to my blessing I will live to see the Church fill its full destiny on the earth, which is to be caught up to meet the Savior at his second coming. So basically, I won't taste of death. That suits me just fine! If, however, the Church *isn't* true, what does the future hold? It just makes life seem so much more uncertain. What is real? What isn't?

I was fascinated and horrified by everything we were finding out; information that had been carefully hidden by Church leaders over the years. Fortunately, not carefully hidden enough; for the information was still available for those who wanted to find it. Still, I didn't want to believe that Mormonism wasn't true. How could I have been duped for so long? Maybe I had been blind to the facts because I *wanted* the Church to be true.

The final straw for me was when I learned that of Joseph Smith Junior's 33 documented wives, 11 of them were currently married to living men.[2] Another 11 of his wives were ages 14 to 20. Several of them were threatened with eternal damnation for them and their families if they refused to become his plural wives, and promised exaltation for them and their families if they consented.[3] I decided if that bit of history could indeed be verified, then I would know that Joseph Smith was not a true prophet of God. I could *somewhat* understand Heavenly Father requiring the practice of polygamy, but for him to condone, let alone command, the taking of other men's wives seemed contrary to everything the gospel stood for. In my mind, there was no way the real God of the universe would violate the sanctity of marriage in that way. But, the evidence for Smith's polyandrous unions was overwhelming.

The foundation of Mormonism quickly unraveled from there. I learned that much of the time Joseph Smith claimed to be translating the Book of Mormon he did not even have the gold plates in his view or possession. Instead, he had a "peep stone" in his hat, which purportedly gave him revelations after putting his face into the hat to block out all light, so he could see what words would appear. This was contrary to what I had been taught in seminary, which is that Smith used a tool called the Urim and Thummim that had been found with the golden plates, along with a breastplate that was to be worn while doing the work of translation.[4] In seminary and Sunday school our teachers told us that the prophet donned the breastplate, put on the spectacles, and pored over every ancient word until the correct corresponding English word appeared. He would then have his scribe write it down. The next word would not appear until the previous one was properly recorded.

However, in actuality, for the work of translation, Smith used a stone he found while helping to dig a well on his neighbor's property several years before claiming to have found the gold plates.[5] The real story was certainly not being taught over the pulpit. From what I knew of the occult, I recognized the practices of channeling and automatic writing, which is what it seemed Smith was involved in.

Many things about the translation of the Book of Mormon from gold plates didn't make sense once I actually thought about it. It seemed more likely that the Book of Mormon was a fictional account. I learned there were many contemporary resources available to Smith to enable him to author the Book of Mormon on his own or possibly with the help of others. The Book of Mormon has themes and passages strikingly similar to the writings of Ethan Smith, who only a few years before wrote *View of the Hebrews*, published in 1823.

Mormon historian B. H. Roberts (1857-1933) found 18 parallels between *View of the Hebrews* and The Book of Mormon that are documented in papers he wrote, which were published in a book entitled *Studies of the Book of Mormon* in 1985. Roberts, a defender of Mormonism, conceded there were many tales in circulation during Smith's early life of Indians being the descendants of Hebrews who migrated to the Americas by ship. Books and articles published before the Book of Mormon speculated that the American Indian was descended from Israelite heritage; *The Wonders of Nature and Providence*, by Josiah Priest in 1824; *The History of American Indians*, by John Adair in 1775; among other written materials by preachers and teachers too numerous to list here.[6] Roberts wrote;

> It will appear in what is to follow that such "common knowledge" did exist in New England; that Joseph Smith was in contact with it; that one book, at least, with which he was most likely acquainted, could well have furnished structural outlines for the Book of Mormon; and that Joseph Smith was possessed of such creative imaginative powers as would make it quite within the lines of possibility that the Book of Mormon could have been produced in that way (Roberts, 1992, p. 154).

I began a regular correspondence with Rauni Higley (H.I.S. Ministries International) in September, asking her questions about how she ended up leaving the Church, and what kind of evidence she could provide to back up her claim that the

Church wasn't true. Even though it appeared obvious that Smith was not a true prophet and that the Book of Mormon, as well as the Book of Abraham in the *Pearl of Great Price*, was fraudulent, the whole prospect felt surreal. Wasn't it possible for the Church to be true while being led by leaders who had gone astray?

Despite my reluctance to admit it, all the evidence was stacking up against Mormonism. With Thanksgiving around the corner, we decided to take a trip to Utah to spend the holidays with family, while taking the opportunity to visit Dennis and Rauni Higley, and Jerald and Sandra Tanner (Utah Lighthouse Ministry). We wanted to meet the people behind the research to hear what they had to say.

One of our nephews arranged for us to talk to his LDS Institute director, Brother Peterson, whom he had a great deal of respect for. Our nephew, Scott, and I drove to Brother Peterson's house and sat at the kitchen table to discuss our concerns about the Church, hoping he would be able to give us good reasons to believe it was true. Scott took out his tape recorder so we could record the conversation. We wanted to be able to listen to it again to make sure we understood him correctly and not wonder about anything we may or may not have heard him say. Brother Peterson told us he didn't want anything on record "because of who he worked for." In other words, the Church was providing him with a paycheck and he didn't want anything to jeopardize his job or standing in the Church.

Scott and I laid out some of our major concerns: the mistranslation of the Book of Abraham, Joseph Smith taking other men's wives, problems with the Book of Mormon—including no archaeological evidence—the testimony of the Three Witnesses prefacing the Book of Mormon, (who later admitted they didn't actually see the gold plates with their physical eyes, but only with their "spiritual eyes"), and the Adam-God doctrine. We were hoping for real answers, ones that would adequately give a reasonable and sound defense of Mormonism; however, this was not to be the case.

Brother Peterson looked us in the eyes and essentially said, "I could be sitting in your place right now. I've had a lot of the same questions you do. What it all comes down to is faith. And really, whether the Church is true or not, it still does good things. It's the best thing out there. The Bible has problems too; it's full of all kinds of contradictions."

We asked him what kind of contradictions, but he couldn't give us a single one. We argued that regardless of whatever problems he thought the Bible may have, it had no bearing on the LDS Church and didn't change the fact that there were major problems with the veracity of Mormon Scripture and the Church's contradictory doctrines. We left the Peterson home more troubled than ever, with our dwindling testimonies of "the gospel" eroding even further. Our nephew, on the other hand, didn't seem to be troubled at all. He seemed just as convinced as ever that the Church was true.

---

1. When my in-laws went through the Temple in 1943, they would have repeated these words for the first token of the Aaronic priesthood: "We, and each of us, covenant and promise that we will not reveal any of the secrets of this, the first token of the Aaronic priesthood, with its accompanying name, sign, or penalty. Should we do so, we agree that our throats be cut from ear to ear and our tongues torn out by their roots." By 1984, the words were changed to "I…covenant that I will never reveal the First Token of the Aaronic priesthood, with its accompanying name, sign, and penalty. Rather than do so, I would suffer my life to be taken." This is said while mimicking the act of slitting one's throat by drawing the right thumb across the neck. In 1990, the words were changed to; "I… covenant before God, Angels, and these witnesses, that I will never reveal the First Token of the Aaronic priesthood with its accompanying name and sign." (Jerald and Sandra Tanner, *Evolution of the Mormon Temple Ceremony: 1842-1990*, (Utah Lighthouse Ministry: Salt Lake City, UT, 1990) 78, 179.
2. "Joseph not only paid his addresses to the young and unmarried women, but he sought 'spiritual alliance' with many married ladies who happen to strike his fancy. He taught them that all former marriages were null and void, and that they were at perfect liberty to make another choice of the husband. The marriage covenants were not binding, because they were ratified only by Gentile laws. These laws the Lord did not recognize; consequently all the women were free.

   "Again, he would appeal to their religious sentiments, and their strong desire to enter into the celestial kingdom. He used often to argue in this manner while endeavoring to convince some wavering or unwilling victim: 'Now, my dear sister, it is true that your husband is a good man, a very good man, but you and he are by no means kindred spirits, and he will never be able to save you in the celestial kingdom; it has been revealed by the Spirit that you ought to belong to me.'

   "This sophistry, strange as it may seem, had its weight, and scarcely ever failed of its desired results. Many a woman, with a kind, good husband, who loved her and trusted her, and a family of children, would suffer herself to be sealed to Joseph, at the same time living with the husband whom she was wronging so deeply, he believing fondly that her love was all his own."

   "One woman said to me not very long since, while giving me some of her experiences in polygamy: 'The greatest trial I ever endured in my life was living with my husband and deceiving him, by receiving Joseph's attentions whenever he chose to come to me.'

   "This woman, and others, whose experience has been very similar, are among the very best women in the church; they are as pure-minded and virtuous women as any in the world. They were seduced under the guise of religion, taught that the Lord commanded it, and they submitted as to a cross laid upon them by the divine will. Believing implicitly in the prophet, they never dreamed of questioning the truth of his revelations, and would have considered themselves on the verge of apostasy, which to a Mormon is a most dangerous and horrible state, from which there is no possible salvation, had they refused to submit to him and to receive his 'divine doctrines." Ann-Eliza Young, *Wife* No. 19, 1876, pp. 70, 71, as cited in *Joseph Smith and Polygamy* by Jerald and Sandra Tanner (Utah Lighthouse Ministry: Salt Lake City) 50-51.

3. Heber C. Kimball offered his 14-year-old daughter, Helen Marr Kimball, to Smith. She agonized for the next 24 hours, but trusted her father. She wrote, "... and no one else could have influenced me at that time or brought me to accept of a doctrine so utterly repugnant and so contrary to all of our former ideas and traditions."

   "The mention of twenty-four hours shows that time pressures were being placed on the prospective bride, just as Smith had applied a time limit to Lucy Walker. The next morning Joseph himself appeared in the Kimball home and personally explained 'the principle of Celestial marrage [sic]' to Helen. In her memoir Helen wrote, 'After which he said to me, "If you will take this step, it will ensure your eternal salvation & exaltation and that of your father's household & all of your kindred. ["] This promise was so great that I willingly gave myself to purchase so glorious a reward.'

   "As in the case of Sarah Whitney, Joseph gave the teenage daughter responsibility not only for her own salvation but for that of her whole family. Thus Helen's acceptance of a union that was not intrinsically attractive to her was an act of youthful sacrifice and heroism." (Todd Compton, *In Sacred Loneliness: The Plural Wives of Joseph Smith* (Signature Books: Salt Lake City, 1997), 498-499.

4. "[T]here was a book deposited, written upon gold plates, giving an account of the former inhabitants of this continent, and the source from whence they sprang... Also, that there were two stones in silver bows—and these stones, fastened to a breastplate, constituted what is called the Urim and Thummin—deposited with the plates; and the possession and use of these stones were what constituted 'seers' in ancient or former times; and that God had prepared them for the purpose of translating the book (*Pearl of Great Price*, Joseph Smith History 1:35).

5. David Whitmer, who was one of the Three Witnesses to the Book of Mormon, wrote, "I will now give you a description of the manner in which the Book of Mormon was translated. Joseph would put the seer stone into a hat, and put his face in the hat, drawing it closely around his face to exclude the light; and in the darkness the spiritual light would shine. A piece of something resembling parchment would appear, and on that appeared the writing..." (*An Address To All Believers In Christ*, Richmond, Missouri, 1887, p. 12).

6. For further study, read the section entitled, *Literature Available to Joseph Smith as a Ground Plan for the Book of Mormon*, pp. 151-161, *Studies of the Book of Mormon*, Second Edition (1992), by B.H. Roberts.

CHAPTER 20

Taking Off the Blinders

Remember, that all I am offering is the truth, nothing more... The truth is that the world you were living in was a lie.

—Morpheus, The Matrix

The ride to Dennis and Rauni's house in the late afternoon was subdued, reflecting our pensive moods. The trees had all but lost their leaves, and the brown barren trunks were in stark contrast to the bright blue sky. Snow capped the tops of the surrounding mountains, and the air was crisp. We stepped out of the van, pulling our coats around us, and walked hand in hand to the doorstep.

"Well, this is it," Scott said, his breath forming wispy vapors that quickly dissipated. "This is where we find out if the Church is true or not."

"No," I replied glumly, "This is where *you* find out the Church isn't true. I'm already pretty sure it's not."

We rang the doorbell. Within seconds the door was opened by a pleasant-looking couple. They greeted us warmly, taking our coats and inviting us to sit down in their comfortable living room with a vaulted ceiling and tall windows. Beautifully carved woodwork and trim adorned the room. We learned that Dennis was a businessman by trade, but woodworking was his beloved hobby and had done the work himself. After losing his retail and other businesses due to leaving the Church, he turned his hobby into an income source. His slogan was, "My

Boss is a Jewish Carpenter: I Follow Him in Everything." A colorful parrot sat on a perch in the corner, staring at us curiously and letting out an occasional squawk.

For the next seven hours we sat enrapt as the Higley's told us their account of leaving Mormonism. Dennis was raised a sixth-generation Mormon, with ancestors going back to the days of Joseph Smith. When the Church called him to serve a two-year mission in Finland, he was eager to go and thankful for the opportunity to stay an extra six months when asked. While in Finland, he met his future wife who was a convert to the Church and serving a mission there in her homeland. She was released from her mission before Dennis and immediately moved to Salt Lake City to live among other Mormons and work for the LDS Church.

The Church hired Rauni as a translator and interpreter. This was a fulltime job and included translating lesson manuals, general conferences, and all other materials that were part of the Church's world-wide goal of spreading Mormonism in every language. Translation is a rather involved process. One word can have a variety of meanings depending on its context. In order to give the most accurate translation, Rauni had to read full articles, sermons, and writings of Church leaders past and present to make sure every nuance was understood before choosing the right words. She was given access to the Church's archives, where volumes of published and unpublished writings were kept.

Over the next 14 years, as Rauni continued her work as a translator, she became more and more troubled by the material in the archives. She found many conflicting doctrines and teachings, as well as historical records that had been revised to keep embarrassing information from harming the Church's reputation.

Rauni told us that when she went through the temple for the first time in Switzerland as a young woman, she also went through the ceremonies vicariously for her deceased mother that same day. She thought it was strange to be receiving promises of health and strength for someone who was dead. She made vows in behalf of her mother that she would wear the sacred garments day and night for the rest of her life, which didn't make sense. How could all the dead people who were having temple work done on their behalves be making covenants to do things that could only apply to living mortals on this earth? Nevertheless, Rauni swept those questions "under the rug," as many Mormons do when confronted by uncomfortable or confusing information.

Translating the temple ceremony from English into Finnish really brought all Rauni's doubts to a head. She realized that at every important juncture in the temple—whether in the movie or in the live reenactment—it was the character of

Satan who called the shots and gave the orders. When "Adam" prayed to God, it was Lucifer who came forth and answered his prayer. After Adam and Eve partook of the forbidden fruit, Satan instructed them to make aprons of fig leaves to cover their nakedness. For the rest of the temple ceremony Adam and Eve, and patrons there in the temple, wear a fig leaf embroidered apron over their temple clothes. Mormons are married and buried wearing the apron. Why would Church members be following Satan's orders instead of God's?

Another thing that bothered Rauni was that the character of Satan wore an apron representing his "power and priesthoods." His apron had the same markings on it that all faithful Mormons have on their temple undergarments. She concluded that the whole temple ceremony, along with the clothing, was satanic in origin and practice; but she kept her thoughts to herself.

Dennis accepted some business opportunities in Vernal, Utah, a little over three hours away. When Rauni told the Church they were moving, they asked her to continue her translation work. Dated (urgent) materials, such as letters from General Authorities, had to be translated within 24 hours. They were sent to her in the evening by Greyhound bus. Rauni translated them and returned them to Salt Lake City the following morning by the same method. During General Conference time twice a year, the Church would provide a room for Rauni in the Hotel Utah for a couple weeks while she translated the talks and other materials into Finnish. By that time she had already concluded Mormonism wasn't true, but with no other religious background or knowledge, she continued attending because she felt it was a "good organization" to belong to.

One day a friend, who worked in the translation department with Rauni before leaving Mormonism, dropped by their house to leave a set of Chuck Missler's (Christian author and teacher) Bible study tapes on the gospel of John. Rauni listened to them and began to understand that not only is God real, but that it matters what a person believes about Him. Soon afterward, while visiting the home of friends who had become inactive in the Church, Rauni found a book by Jerald and Sandra Tanner in their bathroom, outlining the major problems of Mormonism. Rauni was thrilled. She thought she was all alone. Up until then she didn't know that other Mormons had figured out what the real history of the Church was.

Rauni drove to Salt Lake City to the Tanner's bookstore, buying everything that was available. After finishing *Mormonism: Shadow or Reality*, she went to Dennis with her concerns. Night after night he came home from work, and his wife would open up the blue paper-bound book to show him another discrepancy or doctrinal problem. Dennis wanted nothing to do with it, becoming increasingly agitated. Finally he agreed—with the intention of proving Rauni wrong—to look into everything she said, but only from Mormon sources.

Dennis went to a local Mormon bookstore and spent a lot of money to add to their already large collection of LDS books. Rauni read him something from *Shadow or Reality*, and Dennis looked it up in the corresponding LDS book to read it in context. They started one evening after dinner, and by 2 a.m. Dennis stood up, closed the last book, and concluded there were many reasons to suspect that Mormonism was false. He determined to continue his studies in earnest.

At that time, members could not simply resign from the Church and have their names taken off the records. Members had to go through a formal Church court and be excommunicated. Within 24-hours of the Higley's telling their bishop they were leaving the Church, false rumors began to circulate that Dennis was a polygamist with seven wives. At the time, the Higley's were quite wealthy. They owned three businesses in the 85-percent LDS community of Vernal: a small-scale retail department store, a real estate company, and a home-building enterprise. During stake conference, hundreds of members were advised not to do business with the Higley's anymore. Soon, they lost everything they owned, including their home.

When Dennis and Rauni finished telling Scott and me what had happened to them, they took us into their personal library and showed us evidences that Mormonism wasn't true from the Church's own publications. They showed us how the name "Nephi" had been changed to "Moroni" in Joseph Smith's story of the First Vision. We read the "Explanatory Introduction" in the *Doctrine & Covenants* (pre-1981 editions) where it says, "Joseph Smith received visitations from Moroni, an angel of light…" Then Rauni opened up the book *Mormon Doctrine* by LDS Apostle Bruce R. McConkie (1966, p. 35), where under the term "Angel of Light" it says "See Devil." They referenced the Bible where Satan is referred to as an "angel of light" (2 Corinthians 11:14-15).

The Higley's showed us where Smith wrote he had "a constitutional right to be a false prophet, as well as a true one" (Teachings of the Prophet Joseph Smith, p. 344). Smith also boasted;

> As Paul boasted, I have suffered more than Paul did… If they want a beardless boy to whip all the world, I will get on top of the mountain and crow like a rooster: I shall always beat them. Come on! ye prosecutors! ye false swearers! All hell, boil over! Ye burning mountains, roll down your lava! for I will come out on the top

at last. I have more to boast of than ever any man had. I am the only man that has ever been able to keep the whole church together since the days of Adam. A large majority of the whole have stood by me. Neither Paul, John, Peter, nor Jesus ever did it. I boast that no man ever did such a work as I. The followers of Jesus ran away from Him; but the Latter-day Saints never ran away from me yet... How I do love to hear the wolves howl! When they can get rid of me, the devil will also go (History of the Church, Vol. 6, pp. 408-409).

The scales were falling from our eyes, and any illusion we wished to maintain that the Church was true melted away. The question now became: If Mormonism isn't true, what is? What could be trusted? What was real? The Higley's were adamant that the Bible was trustworthy, reliable, and "translated correctly." They gave us a full, detailed Bible study of the gospel of John so we could listen and learn the truth about who Jesus really was when he walked the earth some 2,000 years ago.

Loading our arms with videocassettes, books, and pamphlets for further study, Dennis and Rauni sent us on our way at almost one in the morning. Everything seemed so clear; there was no way on God's green earth that the Mormon Church could be true. After weeks of inner turmoil, struggle, and uncertainty we finally had answers to our many questions and felt a great sense of relief, albeit coupled with sorrow.

The next morning we visited Jerald and Sandra Tanner's bookstore. The infamous "apostates" were very gracious; not at all like the villains they were portrayed to be by Church leaders. We left with an armload of books and free materials. At this rate it would take ages to read through it all. I read aloud as we drove. Every few minutes I would exclaim, "Oh. My. Gosh. You've got to be kidding!"

One example was a major contradiction of doctrine. Section 1 of the 1835 Doctrine and Covenants was titled "Theology or Doctrine of the Church of Latter-day Saints." In Lecture V of that section, Smith wrote that *"there are two personages in the Godhead, and they are the Father and the Son: The Father being a personage of spirit...and the Son a personage of tabernacle, made, or fashioned like unto man..."* The Holy Ghost is not mentioned in this lecture, only the Holy Spirit, and he is said to be *"the mind of the Father and the Son."*[1]

Note that the *Holy Ghost* in Mormonism is a Spirit Person; a son of God, and a third person of godhead. He, like the Father and the Son, can only be present in one place at one time.[2] However, the *Holy Spirit* is described as an influence of God and it can be everywhere present.[3]

127

If Smith had really seen the Father and Son in 1820, he would have seen that both the Father and the Son had bodies of flesh and bone, as Smith began to teach years later. So why was he teaching that God was a personage of spirit? I found it very interesting that the Lectures on Faith were part of the Doctrine and Covenants up until 1921, when they were removed from future editions. Could it be because those early teachings contradicted later teachings?

We spent another night with family, staying up till three in the morning discussing the implications of everything we had discovered. I had a conversation with my sister-in-law and nephew about Brigham Young teaching the doctrine that Adam was in fact our father and our God. They immediately tried to correct me by saying, "Oh, you mean the Adam-God *theory*. It was just President Young's speculation."

I said, "It was not speculation. He said it was a doctrine that a person had to believe or be damned. He taught it for over 25 years. You've got the Journal of Discourses sitting across the room in the bookcase. I can show you the different sermons where he taught Adam is God."

They told me they didn't need to look. I insisted, but they declined. Finally, they told me it would be a lack of faith on their part if they looked in the Journal of Discourses to see if I was right. That's when I decided they'd been brainwashed, when they couldn't even objectively look at the facts out of fear or blind loyalty; I wasn't sure which.

In another conversation my brother-in-law stated that he didn't care if 90% of the members and leadership left the Church; he would remain faithful until the end. I realized with great sadness that just as you can lead a horse to water but can't make it drink, you can lead someone to truth, but can't make him think. If the president of the Church were to stand up in General Conference and declare that the Church was founded on fraud and deception, there would be a percentage of members who would still cling to Mormonism by rationalizing he was a fallen prophet who had been led astray.

Scott asked one of his brothers if he knew anything about the Book of Abraham being mistranslated or about Joseph Smith marrying other men's wives. Before he could get any further, his brother told him if he would just clean up his life and become worthy, get his temple recommend, and live the gospel to the fullest, he could pray and get a testimony that the Church is true. In other words, don't pray to find out what the truth is, but keep praying to know that the Church is true and don't stop asking until you can talk yourself into believing it. That's essentially what happened the first Sunday of each month in *Fast and Testimony Meeting*. As members we took turns at the podium repeating variations of the theme (almost a mantra) "I know the Church is true…," like we were all trying to keep convincing ourselves and others.

As we packed the van for our trip home to Las Vegas, I overheard my 10-year-old nephew warning our soon-to-be eight-year-old son, "Your mom is never going to let you be baptized [as a Mormon] because she's an apostate now." How in the world does a 10-year-old even know what an apostate is?

I explained to Trevor that we were learning some things about the Church that weren't quite right, and we would have to do some more study before letting him get baptized. I told him we had to do the right thing even if everyone else thought we were wrong.

---

1. Wilford C. Wood, *Joseph Smith Begins His Work, Vol. 2* (Wilford C. Wood Publisher: United States of America, 1958). This statement can also be found in the stand-alone volume of the Lectures on Faith, p. 65.
2. Bruce R. McConkie, *Mormon Doctrine* (Bookcraft: Salt lake City, UT, 1966), 359
3. Ibid. pp. 752-753

CHAPTER 21

You Can't Fire Me;
I Quit!

This is your last chance. After this, there is no turning back. You take the blue pill, the story ends; you wake up in your bed and believe whatever you want to believe. You take the red pill, you stay in Wonderland and I show you how deep the rabbit-hole goes.

—Morpheus, The Matrix

Our whole world was in an uproar. As far as the kids were concerned, the family was falling apart, and we were going to hell in a hand-basket. It was a time of great confusion for them. Our youngest three children, ages six, three, and newborn, were too young to understand any of what was going on. The other seven kids, ages 8, 10, 12, 14, 16, 18, and 20, were extremely worried and upset. All their lives they had been taught that Mormonism was true—the only true religion on the face of the earth—and that they could have testimonies of its truthfulness simply by praying for a warm feeling about it. All their lives they been taught to rely on their feelings, which they were told were the promptings of the Spirit. For every other subject—history, politics, mainstream media, and public education—we taught them to think and be critical, to not believe everything they heard, but to research things out. Sadly, in the very thing that mattered most (religion), we had told them to rely on subjective emotions.

As soon as we got back to Las Vegas, I began to prepare for the lesson I would be teaching two weeks later, December 10th. It was the last Relief Society lesson I would ever teach. I couldn't leave the Church without at least trying to warn people. It was still a scary time for me. I wasn't yet bold enough to come right out in public and declare Mormonism to be false. I don't know what I was afraid of. Maybe it was because all I had ever known was Mormonism, and all my closest relationships were within the Church. I knew that once I severed those ties, I would feel like a ship lost at sea with no one on board except me. My kids were threatening mutiny, jumping overboard into lifeboats and sailing away toward the "Mormon harbor." I felt very alone. Even though Scott had come to the conclusion that Mormonism couldn't be true, he had a difficult time letting go of it. It was his heritage, his tradition, and the very way he defined himself. He was more scared than I was.

I decided to prepare the Relief Society lesson on the topic *Beware of False Prophets*. I met with my two counselors, Karen and Michelle, for the last time we would meet as a presidency. They could tell something was different about me. They tried to pry it out of me, but all I would tell them is that they would find out on Sunday. Worried, they went to the Bishop and told him something was wrong. They thought maybe I was struggling with my testimony, although I seemed very adamant about teaching the upcoming lesson.

Bishop Lytle told one of his counselors to sit in on the lesson, observe, and report back. I focused on Deuteronomy chapters 13 and 18, in which the Lord instructed the people of Israel how to discern a false prophet;

> **Deuteronomy 13:1-3**; If a prophet or someone who gets messages while dreaming arises among you and he gives you a sign or wonder, and a sign or wonder comes about as he predicted when he said, "let's follow other gods, which you have not known; and let us serve them," you are not to listen to what that prophet or dreamer says. For *ADONAI* (Hebrew for "Lord") your God is testing you, in order to find out whether you really do love *ADONAI* your God with all your heart and being (*CJB*).

> **Deuteronomy 18:21-22**; You may be wondering, 'How are we to know if a word has not been spoken by *ADONAI*?' When a prophet speaks in the name of *ADONAI*, and the prediction does not come true – that is, the word is not fulfilled – then *ADONAI* did not speak that word, the prophet who said it spoke presumptuously; you have nothing to fear from him (*CJB*).

I read Matthew 24:11, in which Jesus warned that in the end times "many false prophets will appear and fool many people." I told the ladies in class that it was very important to hold fast to the Bible, to study it, and trust it. I told them that truth must be measured against the yardstick of biblical Scripture, and that if anyone taught doctrines contrary to what the Bible teaches, we could know it was false. During the lesson, one of my counselors kept interjecting that we should follow our Church's prophets, and I kept reemphasizing that the Bible is God's word and we should rely on it alone.

When the lesson was over, several of the ladies came up and hugged me, telling me how much they enjoyed it. The Bishop's counselor, Brother Patterson, shook my hand after class and complimented me on doing such a great job. He told me he felt prompted by the Spirit to ask me to speak in Sacrament meeting the following week. I'm not sure which spirit prompted him, but I don't think it was the spirit of discernment, seeing how I was about to leave the Church for good.

That afternoon I called Bishop Lytle and asked if he could come to our house because I had something important to tell him. With the Bishop sitting across from me I said, "There is no simple way to put this, so I'll just come out and say it. I need to be released as Relief Society president because I don't believe the Church is true. In fact, I *know* it isn't true."

"What's going on?" Bishop Lytle looked genuinely concerned. "I was afraid it was something like this when Sister Taylor and Sister Fonbuena called me and told me they were concerned about you. That's why I asked Brother Patterson to sit in on your lesson."

"Yeah, he really enjoyed it. He liked the lesson so much he asked me to speak in Sacrament meeting next Sunday." I had to keep myself from grinning.

"Well, you know I can't let you do that."

"I figured."

The Bishop turned to Scott and asked him how he felt about what was going on. Scott explained that he had a lot of questions himself, and just didn't see how the Church could be true.

"Have you been going to the temple?" Bishop Lytle asked me.

"I haven't been lately," I answered, "not in the last couple months. And I'm not wearing my [temple] garments anymore. I haven't worn them for about a month. I guess you'll want my temple recommend back."

"Yes, I'll need that back."

I went into my room, retrieved my temple recommend from my wallet, came back and handed it to the Bishop. "I have something else to give you too." I handed him a folded piece of paper in an envelope. "It's my resignation letter. I want my name taken off the records of the Church."

"Whoa now, Sister, this is serious. Are you sure you want to do this?"

"I'm surer about this than anything else I've ever been sure of."

"I really don't want to do this, Sister Crookston. Will you let me hang onto this letter for a while before I turn it in? I'd like you and Brother Crookston to get with your home teacher and do some studying with him. I'll talk with him first to make sure it's okay. Will you do this for me? I'm asking you as your friend."

"I suppose, when you put it like that. I can wait for the sake of our friendship." We shook hands and the Bishop left, taking my resignation letter with him, which read as follows:

Dear Bishop Lytle,

This is to inform you that as of today, November 29, 2000, I have terminated my membership in the Church of Jesus Christ of Latter-day Saints.

1. Please remove my name from the records of the Church.
2. In 30 days please send me a letter confirming that my membership was terminated *at my request.*
3. The word "excommunication" is not to be used in your letter to me, nor on the record.

At this time I would like to express my appreciation for your example, outstanding character, and kindness. You are truly a wonderful man, and I have valued your friendship. I hope that our friendship will continue, although I understand if it cannot.

The reason for my leaving the Church is that I was ignorant of its history and many un-biblical doctrines. As an investigator at age 13, I failed to *investigate.* Had I known at that time what I know now, I would not have joined the LDS Church. The history and doctrines that have caused me particular concern and distress are as follows:

- Joseph Smith practicing polyandry and polygamy and attempting to enforce it by the threat of eternal damnation if refused.
- Joseph Smith changing his accounts of the First Vision numerous times; in one account he claimed to have seen one personage, in another he claimed to have seen two. In still another there was no mention of any personages, only angels. In the *Fifth Lecture on Faith* Joseph teaches that God the Father

is a Spirit, and not of flesh and bone. Which account are we to believe?

- Brigham Young teaching that the Savior's Infinite Atonement is *finite*. He taught the principle of "blood atonement;" the necessity of shedding one's blood for sins like adultery—sins which Jesus clearly forgave during his lifetime, and clearly forgives now.
- Brigham Young preaching for over 25 years the heresy of Adam being God the Eternal Father and the only God with whom we have dealings with. Wilford Woodruff and John Taylor also taught that as doctrine.
- Brigham Young, Orson Pratt, Bruce R. McConkie, Ezra Taft Benson and many other leaders teaching that Jesus was not born of a Virgin, but rather the product of a physical, earthy union of God the Father and Mary.
- Gordon B. Hinckley stating in a *Time Magazine* interview that he does not know that the Church teaches "As man is God once was, as God is man may become."
- Gordon B. Hinckley admitting that the Christ followed by the Mormons is not the Christ followed by traditional Christianity.
- *The Book of Abraham* in the *Pearl of Great Price* being a bogus translation. Joseph Smith claimed that the papyrus he translated had been the original parchment written by the hand of Abraham himself, and up until 1967 the Church taught that as well. In 1967 the LDS Church gave the parchment to BYU scholars and other certified Egyptologists to verify the translation, only to find that it is a Pagan funerary ritual taken from the *Book of Breathings / Book of the Dead*.
- The LDS Church and its leaders making changes to Church history, suppressing evidence, and disciplining those with the courage to speak out.

The list could go on and on, and if you wish to know more, I will be happy to show you *in the Church's own history and writings* the above information and much more.

Being the caring person you are, I am sure you are concerned about my eternal welfare and that of my family. I would like to express at this time my assurance to you that I know what I am doing, as God has led me to the truth after many months of prayer, study, and searching the Bible for the answers.

I have never felt happier than I do now, now that I know my Savior. He is NOT the spirit brother of Satan. Jesus is the CREATOR of ALL THINGS, including Lucifer (John 1:3, Col. 1:16). God does not have a father who had a father, ad infinitum, neither does Jesus have His beginning as a spirit child of Heavenly Father, for the Bible teaches us that God is "from everlasting to everlasting" (Psalms 90:2, Isaiah 9:6, Hab. 1:12).

I have prayed that the Lord would remove the scales from my eyes and help me to see the truth. He has taught me and cradled me in His ever-merciful arms over the last few weeks and I am seeing things with "new eyes." I am humbled to tears to know that GOD HIMSELF became a man to save us from sin, not by any works we can do, but by His grace alone. He is not our brother; He is our GOD. I worship, praise, and adore Him.

Through this whole process, even when everything seemed to crumble around me as I discovered that the LDS Church is not true, I have felt a peace and a comfort that I have never experienced as a "worthy temple-recommend holding" Mormon. I have given 26 years to a false church, but I am not bitter; I have nine precious children to show for it.

May you have the courage to SEEK the truth and not just accept blindly what is taught by the Church. If the Church is indeed true, it should hold up under scrutiny. If not, the sooner you find out, the better off you will be.

Your friend,
Tracy Crookston

Scott and I waited for our home teacher to call us and set up a weekly appointment to go over the issues with him. In the meantime, I began looking for a church where biblical truth was taught.

CHAPTER 22

Family Survival

"Mom, are we going to hell?" Trevor looked at me, his eyebrows knit together in concern. "I mean for listening to that music in church. They had drums and guitars. Isn't that wrong?"

"It's not wrong, sweetie, it's just different. I know it's kind of weird, but we'll get used to it," I tried to reassure him.

"It just doesn't seem right," Trevor said as we began walking across the parking lot toward home, a few blocks away.

"We'll just keep looking until we find a church we're comfortable at. The important thing is that they teach the truth about God." It was the first time in probably 30 years that I'd gone to a Christian church as a non-Mormon. Because of our music connections, Scott and I were sometimes invited to a Christian church to sing a special song as part of the service. Whenever we had that opportunity I always chose a Mormon song that communicated some of our doctrines. Even if the audience didn't know what was going on (and I suspect they didn't), we felt we were at least planting seeds so they would eventually accept the Mormon gospel.

This time I wasn't in a Christian church as an undercover missionary; I was there as part of the congregation, coming to be fed by God's word. I was definitely fed. I don't remember much about the sermon, but I remember being deeply touched by most of the music. All the songs were centered on Jesus, His love for us, His blood that was shed for our sins, and our adoration and love for Him. Instead of hymnals, the words to the songs were projected onto large screens in the sanctuary. When we sang *Lord, I Lift Your Name on High,* I choked up after the first few lines. Before the song was over, tears were streaming down my cheeks. What a difference between these Christian lyrics that glorified God and the LDS hymns that—more often than not—glorified the Church, the LDS prophets, or Joseph Smith.

Over the next few weeks I visited at least four different churches on Sundays and mid-week services, ranging from non-denominational to Four-Square to Baptist. Each time, I went directly to the information desk (and after service to the pastor) and introduced myself; "Hi, I'm Tracy Crookston. I just left the Mormon Church." Jaws would drop, followed by big smiles, hearty handshakes, and warm welcomes. Some people expressed surprise because they didn't think *anyone* left Mormonism, or that it was extremely rare.

During the weeks of my search, people from the churches I visited called me to ask if I needed anything or if they could help in any way. I thanked them and said I would appreciate their prayers as I looked for a church for our family. Two surprising things happened.

First, people would ask to pray for me right then and there over the phone. Was that allowed? I mean, really; was that okay with God? I didn't know if I should hold the phone between my ear and shoulder, fold my arms, and close my eyes (and hope I didn't get a kink in my neck), or if I could just hold the phone in my hand and fold one arm. Could I remain standing or did I need to kneel? I was flabbergasted when they told me that God listens to our prayers whether we're on the phone or not, kneeling or standing, eyes open or shut. In addition, they prayed in everyday colloquial language instead of formal King James English. It felt as if they knew God personally and had an intimate relationship with Him. That was pretty cool.

Second, the people who called told me they were happy I visited their church and hoped I would come back, but that there were many good churches around and they wished me the best. At different services I heard pastors say the same thing; they welcomed visitors, said they hoped they would become part of their congregation, but went on to say there were many good churches in the area. In fact, several of the pastors from various denominations got together for lunch on a monthly basis to discuss issues they faced and how to make their churches and community stronger. That was amazing to me. In Mormonism I was taught that all the churches were arguing among themselves, competing for members, and that each denomination thought they alone had the truth. I found it wasn't like that at all.

One day I was talking with someone from one of the churches I visited, explaining to them that we just weren't used to so much contemporary music in a worship service. It was too much change too soon. The lady told me I should consider trying a Baptist church because they were generally more conservative in style. I looked through the phone book and saw a listing for Shadow Hills Baptist Church. I went to their website and liked what I saw, so that next Sunday I took the six younger kids with me to see what it was like. There was a special building designated just for children's ministry, and even a nursery for babies. A kindly older lady gently took my one-month-old son into her arms and sat down in a rocking chair with him.

The main service was awesome! An inspirational choir sang a mix of hymns and contemporary worship songs, which brought tears to my eyes. The pastor, Michael Rochelle, was so cool. He was down-to-earth, personable, and his message went right to the heart. The printed program actually had message notes with little fill-in-the-blanks. I'd never seen such a thing at church. Pastor Rochelle went from one Scripture to another, expounding the word of God. My spirit soared. When the service was over I stepped outside where Curran and Ammon came running across the courtyard with big grins on their faces.

"Mom! This place is so cool! We love it!" Both of them kept interrupting each other to tell me all about what they learned in class. We went to the children's building to get the younger kids, and then to the nursery to retrieve our baby. He was contently sleeping in the arms of the same woman who took him from me. I don't think she put him down once during the whole service.

"It looks like we found our church-home," I said, as we piled into our minivan. It was truly a good day; a *very* good day.

Curran and Ammon—ages 12 and 11—began to attend Shadow Hills somewhat regularly, while going less frequently to the ward activities. Curran was picking up on quite a bit from overhearing conversations between his dad and me. He began seeing that many things about Mormonism just didn't make sense. He also felt uncomfortable with his first (and last) annual bishop's interview.

When Curran turned 12, he became a deacon in the Aaronic priesthood, with the responsibility of passing the Sacrament (bread and water) to ward members during the Sacrament service. From the age of 12, the youth are expected to have a yearly interview with the bishop to determine their worthiness and assure they are in good standing with the Church. During these interviews, bishops ask some very personal questions about sexual behavior. Curran said it seemed to him that if there was an issue it should be between himself and God, not between himself and the bishop. He was especially put off when the bishop asked some probing questions, looked at him sternly, and basically said; "I have the power of discernment, so don't lie or try to hide anything."

At our new church the kids were learning that sins needed to be confessed to God, and that forgiveness came through Jesus alone and did not have to be dispensed through the medium of human agents. I began incorporating this and other biblical teachings into our daily "family goals" routine.

Up until I left the Church, family goals consisted of singing a hymn, family prayer, reading from the Book of Mormon, reciting the 13 Articles of Faith, memorizing the names of Ray and Marvel Crookston's 16 children and their descendants (at the time there were 101 grandchildren; I think there are now 104), family business, and compliments. Each person had a special day of the week. On their special day they got to offer the prayer, be the first to read Scripture, lead the music, and be complimented. Everyone had to say something they liked about the person.

For example;

>"I like dad because he gives us candy and tells jokes."
>"I like Mom because she cooks for us and is a good singer."
>"I like Summer because she's nice to her brothers."

If someone couldn't think of anything they liked about the sibling (maybe some offense had occurred), they had to say something nice the person did that week, like, "I thought it was nice that Quinn didn't hog all the dessert tonight."

After I left the LDS Church, those basic traditions remained the same, only we substituted a song from a Christian hymnal, read from the Bible instead of the Book of Mormon, and recited the Ten Commandments rather than the 13 Articles of Faith. Still, it was not smooth sailing. The family was in an upheaval. As far as the four oldest kids were concerned, Mom was way off the deep-end and Dad was very confused. More often than not our family goal time ended in disaster with me and one or more of the children in tears.

When it was my turn to read from the Bible, I used the New International Version instead of the King James Version we had all been used to. I remember the first time I walked into a Christian bookstore as a new believer. I saw a man looking at Bibles with his daughter. Walking up to him I said, "Excuse me. I'm a new Christian. I just left Mormonism and want to get anything but the King James, because that's all we used. Could you tell me which one," I paused, searching for the right words, "which version is translated correctly? Which one is the most accurate?"

The man said he preferred a thought-for-thought version, and pointed me to a pamphlet that explained the various Bible translations and their differences.[1] After reading the pamphlet to choose the best version, I came home with my first non-King James Bible ever, which was enough to cause some commotion during family Scripture time. The kids had been taught all their lives that the Bible wasn't translated correctly and didn't have the same accuracy as the Book of Mormon, Doctrine and Covenants, and the Pearl of Great Price. We taught them that the King James—although not translated correctly, according to Mormon teaching—was the most reliable version of all the Bibles. They could barely trust the KJV, and now their "apostate mother" was using some weird modern version.

Despite everyone's skepticism, I loved my new Bible. I literally spent hours each day reading. I couldn't get enough of it. And with all the things I was learning from listening to commentaries on tape from a variety of Bible teachers, my soul was on fire for God! The first thing I wanted to do when I woke up in the morning was open my Bible. The last thing I wanted to do before falling asleep at night was read from my Bible.

As a Mormon I thought the Bible was one of the most boring books ever, especially the Old Testament. It was hard for me to read through it, let alone understand it. But now, since being "born from above" (in other words, since putting my trust in Jesus of the Bible and being spiritually transformed by the Holy Spirit), the Bible came to life for me. It became the most exciting book I had ever read.

Unfortunately, not everyone else in the family felt the same way. As we read aloud, I would stop to explain from the study notes what certain verses meant and what the background and context was for each passage of Scripture. However, it never failed; as soon as I pointed out that Mormon teaching contradicted the plain meaning of the text, Scott would jump in to defend the Mormon view. He would always begin by saying, "Not to play the devil's advocate, *but...*" But that's exactly what he was doing; being an advocate for the Devil. We argued over doctrine until I got so frustrated I'd burst into tears.

"You don't even believe the Church is true! So why do you keep defending it? You're not the one studying. You don't even read Scripture or listen to Bible studies every day, so how do you even know what you're talking about?"

"Well," Scott explained, "I'm just trying to present the other side."

"The kids already know the other side. We've freaking brainwashed them with 'the other side' ever since they were born! Now it's time for them to hear the truth."

By this time our 15-year-old daughter would be crying. "I don't even know why we have family goals anymore. I *hate* family goals! All we ever do is end up arguing!"

"That's what a false religion does, Summer," I would quip, "It destroys families."

"So, who wants to pray?" Scott would then blurt out, ever being the one determined to lighten things up (at the most inappropriate times).

Thus, for months our family devotion time turned into family demolition time. I wondered if our family unit would survive.

---

1. Some Bibles are word-for-word translations. Others are paraphrases. Some Bibles are designed for devotional reading, while others are targeted on study. The better translations are those that closely adhere to the English equivalent of the original Hebrew and Greek words. Bad translations are those that attempt to be politically correct by neutralizing all gender references, or that take great liberties in paraphrasing to the extent that the original *meaning* of the text is lost.

CHAPTER 23

No Middle Ground

Look at 'em. Automatons. Don't think about what they're doing or why. Computer tells 'em what to do and they do it.

—Anthony, The Matrix

We sat down at the executive style conference table in the High Priest Group's room at church, each with a pile of books and notepads in front of us. We met once a week with our home teacher Ken Ellis (name changed), a respected attorney and admired friend, to study the problems of Mormonism. Scott and I naively expected that our home teacher would be able to be objective, using his knowledge and skills as a lawyer to delve into the truth of a matter.

Bishop Lytle's goal was to clear up the issues and keep us in the Church. My goal was to help our friend "see the light." Scott's goal was to see if there was any way possible Mormonism could somehow still be true, because he really wanted it to be.

"Before we start," Ken stated, "I want to make sure my name doesn't end up on some website or in some book down the road."

"Agreed," I responded.

"Then let's proceed." Ken opened to the Table of Contents in *Major Problems of Mormonism* by Jerald and Sandra Tanner. "Why don't we just take one subheading a week? We can do our own research and then discuss what we found."

That sounded good to us. The first week we touched on chapter one, which was only about three pages long and covered some of the incredible claims of the LDS Church. One such claim made in 1892 by Oliver B. Huntington was that almost all the great discoveries of the 19th Century directly or indirectly proved Joseph Smith, Jr. was a prophet.[1]

Smith claimed to have received a revelation that the Garden of Eden had originally been located in Jackson County, Missouri. While in Daviess County, Smith found a pile of rocks that he asserted was part of the very altar on which Adam offered sacrifices.[2] I wondered how any of the altar could still be standing after a world-wide flood in Noah's day changed the whole surface of the planet. Interestingly, according to Smith, Noah built his ark in or near Carolina.[3]

Among other claims made by the LDS Church, is the assertion that it is the only true church upon the face of the earth. Mormon Apostle Orson Pratt wrote:

> The gates of hell have prevailed and will continue to prevail over the Catholic Mother of Harlots, and over all her Protestant Daughters; the apostate Catholic [C]hurch with all her popes and bishops, together with all her harlot daughters shall be hurled down to hell..." (Pamphlets by Orson Pratt, p. 112).[4]

This was the crux of the matter: everything boiled down to whether or not the Church was true. It couldn't be anything in-between; either the Mormon Church is the only true church or it is completely false. This statement is not an "either-or fallacy." As Joseph Fielding Smith, 10th president of the Church declared;

> Mormonism, as it is called, must stand or fall on the story of Joseph Smith. He was either a prophet of God, divinely called, properly appointed and commissioned, or he was one of the biggest frauds this world has ever seen. There is no middle ground. If Joseph was a deceiver, who willfully attempted to mislead people, then he should be exposed, his claims should be refuted, and his doctrines shown to be false.[5]

Other leaders made similar claims, also challenging people (members included) to test the veracity of Mormonism;

> **Ezra Taft Benson** (13th president of the Church): "This is not just another Church. This is not just one of a family of Christian churches. This is the Church and kingdom of God, the only true Church upon the face of the earth...."[6]

George Albert Smith (8th president of the Church): "If a faith will not bear to be investigated; if its preachers and professors are afraid to have it examined, their foundation must be very weak."[7]

Brigham Young (2nd president of the Church): "Take up the Bible, compare the religion of the Latter-day Saints with it and see if it will stand the test."[8]

Joseph Smith, Jr.: "I told the brethren that the Book of Mormon was the most correct of any book on earth, and the keystone of our religion...Take away the Book of Mormon and the revelations, and where is our religion? We have none."[9]

Orson Pratt (Mormon Apostle): [The Book of Mormon], "If true, is one of the most important messages ever sent from God to man. If false, it is one of the most cunning, wicked, bold, deep-laid impositions ever palmed upon the world, calculated to deceive and ruin millions who sincerely receive it as the Word of God, and will suppose themselves built upon the rock of truth, until they are plunged, with their families, into hopeless despair.

"Convince us of our errors of Doctrine, if we have any, by reason, by logical arguments, or by the Word of God and we will ever be grateful for the information and you will ever have the pleasing reflections that you have been instruments in the hands of God of redeeming your fellow beings."[10]

The first meeting laid the foundation for the rest of our time together. The task for Brother Ellis, Scott, and me, was to take up Church leaders on their challenges and test the Church of Jesus Christ of Latter-day Saints to see if it held up under scrutiny.

The following week we began looking into plural marriage. There were so many issues regarding the Mormon doctrine and practice of polygamy, it took more than one week to even scratch the surface. The Church has bounced back and forth, publicly reversing itself on the doctrine of plural marriage. In the 1835 edition of the Doctrine and Covenants, section 101:4, it says;

Inasmuch as this church of Christ has been reproached with the crime of fornication, and polygamy: we declare that we believe, that one man should have one wife; and one woman, but one husband, except in the case of death, when either is at liberty to marry again.

The Tanner's sum it up succinctly;

> This statement is very important because the *Doctrine and Covenants* is one of the four standard works of the Mormon Church. This denial of polygamy was printed in every edition of the *Doctrine and Covenants* until the year 1876. At that time the Mormon leaders inserted section 132, which permits a plurality of wives. Obviously, it would have been too contradictory to have one section condemning polygamy and another approving of it in the same book! Therefore, the section condemning polygamy was completely removed from the *Doctrine and Covenants*.[11]

Another contradiction occurs between volumes of LDS Scripture. In the Book of Mormon, Jacob 2:23-24, it says "David and Solomon truly had many wives and concubines, which thing was abominable before me, saith the Lord." Yet, in Doctrine and Covenants 132:39 we read;

> David's wives and concubines were given unto him of me, by the hand of Nathan, my servant, and others of the prophets who had the keys of this power; and in none of these things did he sin against me save in the case of Uriah and his wife; and, therefore he hath fallen from his exaltation, and received his portion; and he shall not inherit them out of the world, for I gave them unto another, saith the Lord.

In addition to contradictions, are discrepancies and outright dishonesty. The revelation regarding plural marriage was allegedly given in 1843, but by that time Smith had already accumulated over two dozen wives. The most disturbing aspect of Smith's polygamous marriages was the fact that 11 of his wives were concurrently married to other men. Brother Ellis seemed pretty nonchalant about it.

Scott shook his head in exasperation and blurted out, "Come on! He was taking other men's wives! Don't you see a major problem with that?"

Brother Ellis shrugged, rubbed his chin, and said, "Well, I *suppose* that would seem inappropriate."

Scott wondered if Brother Ellis would respond so casually if it had been *his* wife who was demanded of by a leader of the Church.

Besides polygamous marriages (both polygyny and polyandry) by a portion of the early Mormons, the Church publicly denied practicing polygamy all the while leaders were engaging in it. After polygamy was outlawed by the Federal Government and LDS President Wilford Woodruff wrote the Manifesto in 1890 (found in the *Doctrine and Covenants*), plural marriages continued to be authorized secretly by the Church. Woodruff attests,

> I, therefore, as President of the Church of Jesus Christ of Latter-day Saints, do hereby, in the most solemn manner, declare that these charges are false. We are not teaching polygamy or plural marriage, nor permitting any person to enter into its practice, and I deny that either 40 or any other number of plural marriages have during that period been solemnized in our Temples or in any other place in the Territory.[12]

Up until about 1904, Church leadership was performing plural marriage ceremonies, and stating under oath in court that they were not.[13]

During the course of our meetings with Brother Ellis, which lasted a couple months, we moved from one topic to another: Church truth claims, polygamy, the mistranslation of the Book of Abraham, changes in the temple ceremony which were initially said to be eternal and unchangeable, the lack of evidence for the Book of Mormon, and prophecies by Joseph Smith that didn't come to pass. We talked about other events that portended doom for Mormon truth claims, such as the Kinderhook Plates, illegal banking, the Mountain Meadows Massacre, the Salamander Letter forgeries, and contradictory First Vision accounts.

Much to our disappointment, our weekly studies with Brother Ellis were going nowhere. No matter how compelling the evidence, he seemed to uncritically dismiss it and sweep it under the rug. When it came to all the eyewitness testimonies in court records or personal diaries about Joseph Smith's and Brigham Young's unethical, illegal, immoral, or dishonest activities, Brother Ellis attributed it to fabrications by people with axes to grind.

In trying to ascertain whether or not a witness was credible, Brother Ellis didn't even pretend to do any research. He would just blithely say something like, "And who was Wesley P. Walters[14] anyway? We really don't know much about him, so I don't think we can rely on him." Then he'd move on to the next topic.

Finally, on June 2, 2001, after months of listening to feeble arguments by Brother Ellis to defend Mormonism, Scott came to the conclusion he could no longer accept the LDS Church as being true. His last wisps of hope that the Church could somehow be proven true slipped out of reach and dissipated into reality. Sunday June 3rd, Scott called the bishop and told him he wanted to be released from all his callings: ward organist, high priest group teacher, and home teacher.

Bishop Lytle apologized to Scott for not being more involved in his struggle, but said the stake president had instructed him to let ward members handle it. Scott and I both thought that President Bingham was probably more concerned about another leader leaving the Church and shaking up the stake than he was about Scott's search for truth. They already lost a Relief Society president; an event that left the ward devastated. The last thing he needed was for one of his bishops to defect. The only recourse left was damage control.

---

1. Huntington also wrote, "As far back as 1837, I know that he [Joseph Smith] said the moon was inhabited by men and women the same as this earth, and that they lived to a greater age than we do, that they live generally to near the age of 1000 years. He described the man as averaging near six feet in height, and dressing quite uniformly in something near the Quaker style." (Jerald & Sandra Tanner, *Major Problems of Mormonism* (1989), 6. As quoted from the LDS Church publication, *The Young Woman's Journal*, Vol. 3, 263-264)
2. Bruce R. McConkie, *Mormon Doctrine* (Salt Lake City: Bookcraft, 1966), 20
3. Jerald & Sandra Tanner, *Major Problems of Mormonism* (Salt Lake City: Utah Lighthouse Ministry, 1989) 6, referencing The Juvenile Instructor, November 15, 1895, 700-701.
4. Ibid. p. 8
5. Joseph Fielding Smith, *Doctrines of Salvation*, Vol. 1, (Salt Lake City: Bookcraft, 1956), 188-189.
6. Ezra T. Benson, (1988) *The Teachings of Ezra Taft Benson* (Salt Lake City: Bookcraft, 1988), 164-165.
7. *Journal of Discourses, Vol. 14, p. 21*
8. *Journal of Discourses, Vol. 16, p. 46*
9. George A. Smith, *History of the Church, Vol. 2,* p. 52; Vol. 6, pp. 408-409 (Salt Lake City: Deseret Book, 1950).
10. Orson Pratt, *The Seer* (Salt Lake City: Utah Lighthouse Ministry, 1853), 15
11. Jerald & Sandra Tanner, *Major Problems of Mormonism* (Salt Lake City: Utah Lighthouse Ministry, 1989) 9
12. D&C, *Official Declaration* #1, known as The Manifesto, 1981 edition, p. 291.
13. Jerald & Sandra Tanner, 1989. *Major Problems of Mormonism* (Salt Lake City: Utah Lighthouse Ministry, 1989) 24-38.
14. Wesley P. Walters, who passed away in 1990, was a pastor of Marissa Presbyterian Church in Marissa, Illinois. Reverend Walters found an original court record of a Bainbridge, New York, trial in 1826, in which Joseph Smith, Jr. was found guilty of the crime of "glass looking." Smith had been

hiring himself out for the purpose of finding buried treasure and lost property using a "peep stone" (which he later claimed to use in "translating" the Book of Mormon). Apparently, one too many people felt ripped-off when Smith was never able to find and deliver the promised treasures, and decided to press charges, to which Smith confessed guilt. Mormon critics of Walters allege the court document was obtained dishonestly. Whether or not that is the case (a straw-man argument), the fact is that the document is authentic and proves that Smith--at least on this occasion--was a conman; casting doubt upon his character, and on the authenticity of the Book of Mormon.

CHAPTER 24

Courting Disaster

Agent Smith: *My colleagues believe that I am wasting my time with you, but I believe you want to do the right thing... We are willing to wipe the slate clean, to give you a fresh start, and all we are asking in return is your cooperation.*

Neo: *You can't scare me with this Gestapo crap. I know my rights. I want my phone call.*

—The Matrix

About midway through the meetings with our home teacher, I decided that the "study" was going nowhere fast. There were so many problems with Mormon historical revisions, doctrinal changes, and discrepancies that we could conceivably be meeting an hour weekly for years. I wrote another request for my name to be removed and gave it to the Bishop:

April 29, 2001
Dear Bishop Lytle,
I am requesting that you send the letter for my name to be removed from the rolls of the Church immediately. If you no longer have a copy I will provide you with another.
I am continuing the weekly study with Scott, and Ken Ellis, but the fact is, I am never coming back to the Mormon Church, and no amount of further study will "prove" to me the Church is true. What God thinks of me is more important than what man thinks of me. He has already shown

me the truth by reason, study, and His Holy Spirit. For me to continue lingering on the Church rolls is to deny God and His truth.

Several people have inferred that my leaving the Church was because:

1. I didn't have a testimony to begin with
2. I wasn't humble enough or "worthy" enough when I prayed to know the truth
3. I was offended
4. I'm doing this for attention
5. I was tired of "living the gospel" and took the easy way out
6. I did not understand the teachings
7. I let anger over certain doctrines fester until it drove me away
8. I lost the "Spirit"
9. Any combination of the above, plus other bizarre reasons

My response to the above:

1. I *did* have a "testimony," but it was from the wrong source, and based on incomplete information.
2. I came to the Lord in tears of humility, only seeking the truth. While not claiming to be near perfect, I was found worthy enough to hold a temple recommend.
3. I was offended once, about 15 years ago, and it didn't stop me from coming to church.
4. Ridiculous assertion.
5. Easy? I wouldn't call it easy to lose almost all your friends, admiration, respect, a position of authority, having your children look at you with pity, and having your extended family pretty much avoid conversations with you at family gatherings.
6. I did understand the teachings and took them seriously. I was not a "Sunday Mormon." I attended Education Week almost yearly, took Book of Mormon study to heart, read and studied many, many teachings and "deep doctrines," and was fully immersed in Mormonism.
7. While the doctrine of polygamy being essential to exaltation bothered me at one time, I pretty much decided that I would understand it in the next life, and would have to just accept it by faith for now. As a matter of fact, all the doctrines that I didn't understand or take a shine to were just put on the back

burner as I plowed ahead in faith.

8.   That *is* true. I lost the Mormon Spirit, but gained the Holy Spirit.

These last few months since leaving the LDS Church have been the best in the last two decades! I have a personal relationship with my Savior Jesus Christ. I no longer worry and wonder where I stand in regard to salvation/exaltation or what my standing is before God. I know exactly where I stand. He has truly given me the "peace that passes all understanding" (Philippians 4:7). I rejoice in the Lord and find refreshment in His word.

Please remove my name from Church records so I can be free from the taint of belonging to a false church.

Still your friend,
Tracy

I didn't hear anything for over five weeks, long past the 30-day waiting policy prescribed in the Church's *Handbook of Instructions*.

One Sunday in early June, the Bishop came over with our home teacher and an envelope in hand. He shook his head sadly and said, "This is not the letter you've been waiting for." My heart sank. Without opening it I knew what it was. I was right; it was a summons to a Church disciplinary court for "apostate activities." The action was sparked by an incident involving my visiting teachers, Kristy S. and Astrid B.

The week before, my visiting teachers asked if they could take me to lunch. Never one to turn down a good meal—especially Mexican food—and perhaps have a chance to show them the errors of Mormonism, I agreed. We talked all through lunch as I shared with them the reasons I was leaving the Church. After the meal we went to the parking garage and got into their car. Kristy pulled out a photocopied article she said she wanted to read to me. So we sat in the hot, sweltering car with no air conditioner, for a good 45 minutes while she read a General Conference talk aloud to me. I suppose she thought she had a captive audience since I was depending on her for a ride home. Astrid sat silently the whole time. When Kristy was finished reading, she looked at me triumphantly and expectantly, as if the talk given by the prophet would be inspirational enough to restore my testimony of the Church.

I thanked Kristy for her care and concern, but said the conference talk didn't change historical facts. It didn't matter how "inspiring" or good someone's speech is if it's built on a false premise. Unable to make headway they took me home. When we pulled into my driveway I asked them to wait because I wanted to give them something. I ran inside and grabbed a several-page document I had typed up a few days before. It was my account of leaving Mormonism. I hadn't thought of giving it to them until I was subjected to almost an hour of listening to Kristy read pro-Mormon material. I thought it was only fair to give them some reading material of my own.

A couple weeks prior to our lunch date, Kristy asked me to read the book of Hebrews in the Bible and tell her what I thought. Presumably, she figured the passages about the priesthood would make me see that the Church was true. I read the entire epistle to the Hebrews and came away more convinced than ever that Mormonism could not possibly be true. It was clear to me that Jesus was the last High Priest we would ever need as a mediator between God and man. In Him, we have all that is needed for reconciliation with the Almighty.

I responded to Kristy by writing her a letter referencing all the Scripture that says we don't need "latter-day prophets" and Aaronic and Melchizedek priesthood-holders in the way Mormonism teaches. I'm guessing one of the visiting teachers turned those two documents over to the bishop, who then concluded I was engaged in "apostate activities" and therefore subject to disciplinary action.

I looked at the bishop, my eyes welling up with tears over the injustice of it all. "If you would have processed my name-removal request back in November instead of holding on to it, this wouldn't be happening. I can't be an apostate when I already resigned my membership. You asked me to wait for the sake of our friendship and now you're betraying me!"

"Now Sister Crookston," the bishop began, "you're telling people in the ward about everything."

"How come," I asked, "it's all right for the visiting teachers to shove their opinions and testimonies down my throat, holding me hostage in a parking garage while they read Mormon propaganda to me, but as soon as I share *my* testimony with them it's a crime?"

The bishop and home teacher reminded me again that a Church court is a "court of love." I said I already knew what the verdict would be at the conclusion of this "court of love"—excommunication. They told me the decision had not yet been made, because they would have to fast and pray over what should be done.

They said the court proceedings would last about three to four hours. With tears streaming down my face, I told them they could see themselves out; then I went to my room and threw myself on my bed sobbing.

After I'd calmed down a bit, I got on the MIT (Mormons in Transition) forum to ask for advice. Someone suggested I contact a woman named Kathy Worthington (now deceased) in Salt Lake City who had a reputation for successfully helping people get their names removed from Church records. Less than an hour after sending her an email she called me and asked if I was willing to take my complaint to the media or pursue legal action.

"You bet!" I replied, believing it was a matter of principle.

Kathy informed me that the Church had no leg to stand on because I had used the words "I am officially terminating my membership" in the resignation letter I gave to the bishop in November. Since I was no longer to be considered a member of the organization, they couldn't excommunicate me. To do so would constitute defamation of character. She instructed me to write a short letter to the bishop reminding him that I am no longer a member and would not hesitate to go to the media or seek legal redress if he proceeded with a Church court. Kathy said she would call LDS headquarters the following morning to advise them of my intent.

The next morning I headed to the bishop's house with a letter in hand, which read:

June 17, 2001
Bishop Lytle;
This letter is to reaffirm that I officially terminated my membership in The Church of Jesus Christ of Latter-day Saints as of November 29, 2000, and that the letter was to be considered my formal resignation.

I will not participate in any Church court proceedings, as I have already resigned as a member and therefore am not subject to disciplinary actions.

I request that you halt all action against me and cease to threaten me further. If you continue with a disciplinary council, I will consider it harassment, as well as slander against my good name. This letter is to inform you that I will not hesitate in seeking legal redress in court or in the media if my name is not immediately removed from Church records *per my previous and continued requests.*

Again, it is to be noted on the record that I *voluntarily requested* my name to be removed, and that I have done no wrong. I trust that you will be prompt in this matter.

Sincerely,

Tracy Crookston

When the bishop answered the doorbell, he was on the phone with President Bingham. He motioned for me to come in and sit down. Ending his call with President Bingham, he sat across from me on the sofa and told me he was awake most of the night struggling over what to do, and that he decided to cancel the Church court. He told me I was "too confused" for it to do any good. He actually seemed disappointed that he wasn't going to go through with it. He explained how it would have been a good opportunity for me to see that an LDS disciplinary court is a court of love, and that I would be able to "feel the love and the power of the priesthood and the Spirit."

I thought it was too much of a coincidence that the same morning Kathy called LDS headquarters in Salt Lake City the Bishop decided to cancel the court; however, just in case it was, I advised him he could expect a call from the membership department and a letter in the mail from Kathy. He immediately looked shocked and hurt. He shook his head and stuttered to find the words to say.

"Sister, I'm just...I can't believe...I'm, I'm very disappointed. I'm disappointed that you would do this. Why didn't you just come to me and say something? I can't believe you thought it was necessary to go outside the Church for this."

Now it was my turn to be shocked. Wasn't it enough that I had given him two resignation letters over the past seven months? Wasn't it enough that I cried when he came over to hand me the letter stating a Church disciplinary court was to be held? Wasn't I clear enough when I sobbed and told him how unfair and unwarranted a disciplinary court was and that he had no grounds on which to hold one? Would he really have changed his mind if I had dropped to my knees and begged him to reconsider? I think not.

The whole scenario didn't make sense to begin with. The day before, he was telling me that the Spirit prompted him to convene a disciplinary court. Then that morning he was telling me the Spirit prompted him not to go through with it. So, which was it? Did "Heavenly Father" not know in advance what was going to happen or did he simply change his mind? Or was the bishop getting false revelations? Either way, too much contradiction was going on.

With his eyebrows furrowed in sorrow, Bishop Lytle continued, "How could you? How could you do this after all I've done for you and your family?"

Not to sound unappreciative, but none of the food assistance we needed for a few weeks when our income dropped came out of his pocket; it came out of organizational funds. What about the tens of thousands of dollars and hours of service we had given to the Church over the years? We gave more and did more for the Church than the Church had ever given to us. Just to be clear, I'm referring to the LDS Church organization, not to individual members who were always willing to lend a hand or help us and each other. The Bishop seemed to be taking my resignation personally. I was simply disassociating myself with an organization, not trying to break off friendships or betray anybody.

He asked me if I was planning on writing a book or putting things on the internet in regard to Mormonism. I told him that what is known as my "exit story" (account of leaving Mormonism) wasn't yet on the internet, but soon would be (Dennis and Rauni Higley asked if I would allow them to put it on their website). I explained that I didn't have any other plans at the time, but couldn't make promises about the future.

Bishop Lytle looked at me and firmly said, "Then I will proceed."

My heart sank. I thought he meant he was going to proceed with the Church court, so I said, "Even God doesn't punish people in advance for something they *might* do in the future. You're elevating yourself above God."

"Sister, why are you attacking me?" He exclaimed.

"I'm not attacking you. I thought you just said you're going to proceed with convening a Church court."

"No, I meant I will proceed with getting your name removed from Church records," Bishop Lytle clarified.

I found it interesting that he considered my remark as attacking him, yet he didn't seem to think twice about attacking me, my character, and my mothering when he told me earlier that morning that he couldn't believe that as a mother I would leave the Church, and that I should think about my children.

I responded by saying, "Wait a minute. As a parent, if you thought the eternal welfare of your children was in danger, you would do the same thing."

He had no reply, other than to say that leaving the Church might be fine for me, but why would I "try to destroy the faith of others?"

I reiterated, "If you discovered that the Church was built on fraud or thought it was endangering the salvation of its members, you would do the same thing if you really cared about them." Again, he had no defense.

I left the Bishop's house somewhat relieved. After all the grief and anxiety I'd experienced trying to leave the Church, I couldn't wait until I received official confirmation that my name had been removed from membership records so I could put it all behind me.

It's kind of ironic. There's a saying among Mormons that "someone can leave the Church, but they just can't leave it alone;" but I was finding out firsthand that people can attempt to leave the Church but the Church just can't leave *them* alone!

CHAPTER 25

Every Silver Lining
Has a Cloud

Morpheus: *I didn't say that it would be easy, Neo. I just said that it would be the truth.*
Neo: *I can't go back, can I?*
Morpheus: *No. But if you could, would you really want to?*

—The Matrix

Each of us has to face the matter—either the Church is true, or it is a fraud. There is no middle ground. It is the Church and kingdom of God, or it is nothing.
—Gordon B. Hinckley's, "Loyalty," *Ensign*, May 2003, 58

About mid-July the bishop dropped off a letter at my house. It was dated June 25th. It said my request for name removal was being processed and I had 30 days to change my mind. As if another 30 days after approximately 210 was going to make a difference. At least it was progress. The only front on which there wasn't much progress was the home-front. My oldest four children weren't convinced that Mormonism wasn't true, and they didn't want to listen to or look at anything that cast the Church in a bad light. Even Quinn, who had been inactive for years, held to the position that the Church was true and I had gone off my rocker. My two middle children were uncertain, but open.

At least my youngest four children and I were blossoming under our new knowledge of God. For the first time in ages we looked forward to Sundays and were excited about church. Everywhere we drove we had Christian CDs playing full blast while we sang along with them. Two of our favorites were *Sunday School Rock* by Carman, and Michael W. Smith's rendition of *Our God is an Awesome God*.

Whenever we'd get home from church we would tell the rest of the family what we learned from the Bible about God, Jesus, and salvation from sin. I'd ask Scott and the older kids about services in the ward and what the talks[1] were about. Their answers were always the same: the temple, tithing, Joseph Smith, the Book of Mormon, or following the Brethren. I would ask (somewhat sarcastically) if anyone there ever had something to say about Jesus. Scott would quip, "Well, they prayed in his name." Eventually they stopped telling me about what happened at the ward on Sunday. As I said, that first year was the hardest.

Almost one year after requesting that my name be formally removed, I received the official letter I'd been waiting for from the LDS Member and Statistical Records Department, dated October 4, 2001. It read;

Dear Sister Crookston,
This letter is to notify you that, in accordance with your request, you are no longer a member of The Church of Jesus Christ of Latter-day Saints. Should you desire to become a member of the Church in the future, the local bishop or branch president in your area will be happy to help you.

Sincerely,
Gregory W. Dodge
Supervisor,
Confidential Records Section

Little by little Summer and Tristan began listening to me and looking things up for themselves. One time we were sitting in Sacrament Meeting (I still went on a few occasions for the sake of the older kids) and one of the speakers said that the [LDS] temple was the Lord's house. I leaned over to Summer and pointed to Acts 7:48, "Howbeit the most High dwelleth not in temples made with hands," and Acts 17:24, "God that made the world and all things therein, seeing that he is Lord of heaven and earth, dwelleth not in temples made with hands." At the time, Summer just glared at me while I smiled triumphantly, but she began to see that Mormon teachings often conflicted with the Bible.

Although the tide was turning, Jeff held fast to his belief in Mormonism. January 9, 2002, Jeff went into the MTC (Missionary Training Center) in Provo, Utah. There he would undergo intensive preparation for two months before being sent to Uruguay for the balance of his two-year term as an LDS missionary. Although I was heartbroken, I told him I was glad he was going for the right reasons and was proud of him for doing what he believed was right, even though I couldn't in good conscience support him in spreading the Mormon gospel. In fact, his mission was financially supported by ward members who wanted to assure that he could serve the Church as a missionary.

While we were in Utah to take Jeff to the MTC, we stayed at the home of relatives. They had posters of Book of Mormon characters, LDS leaders, and various temples on the bedroom walls, along with one popular depiction of Jesus. My three-year-old daughter pointed to each of the Mormon portraits saying, "Mama, I don't like that guy! No, I don't any of them, but I like Jesus." How she knew which pictures were distinctly Mormon is beyond me, but I had to smile.

A couple months later, four of my sons and I went on big adventure. I had posted on the ex-LDS support group message board that I wanted to take a family trip across the country to look for future places to move to. I didn't think Las Vegas was the best place to raise children, especially with billboards of scantily-clad women being advertised along freeways and on taxicabs. With Scott's blessing we decided to do some traveling. Several people from the support group offered to open up their homes to us as we made the journey from Southern Nevada to Washington D.C. This trip has since become one of our fondest family memories.

We stayed with one couple—Les and Charlie—in Denver. They had an odd salad-eating dog named Oreo and a really nice house with a pool table and outdoor Jacuzzi. I remember sitting in the hot Jacuzzi with the kids, surrounded by a couple feet of snow on the ground. We stayed up late into the night sitting around the kitchen table talking about our experiences in Mormonism and how God delivered us from spiritual bondage.

From Denver we drove to Grand Island, Nebraska, slept at a truck stop, and then went on to Omaha and spent the day at the zoo. From Omaha to Des Moines, and from there to Northfield, Minnesota, we stopped at every mall and bookstore we found along the way. We stayed for five days with Steph and Paul's amazing family. I came down with some stomach bug and was sick almost the whole time. For years my dream had been to visit the Mall of America and here I was, too sick to enjoy it. But the kids loved it, and 8-year-old Trevor had fun on the indoor rollercoaster.

During our stay, Paul's brother Marty was visiting. He shared his life story with us, telling us how he had been a drug addict for years until Jesus delivered him from addiction and miraculously changed his life. Later that day, on May 17 at 11:45 p.m., Tristan woke me up to say he was rejecting Mormonism, and was trusting in Jesus of the Bible as Lord and Savior. Two days later Curran followed suit in declaring his belief in the biblical Jesus.

The next stop on our journey was Grand Rapids, Michigan, where we had arranged to stay for two weeks with Glenn and Diana and their four little children. Glenn was the moderator for the online support forum, *Mormons in Transition*. We had a great time sight-seeing, but the best part of our stay was all the visiting and conversations we had with each other and all the new friends we made along the way. Luke Wilson, the director of IRR (Institute for Religious Research), and his gracious and lovely wife Bertha (both who since passed away) also opened their home to us for several nights.

We left Michigan and traveled to Virginia, where we stayed with my dear friend Becky, "The Other Woman" alluded to in previous chapters. It was so good to see her and spend time with her. How grateful I was for the courage and love of others that she demonstrated by looking me up almost two years earlier to share her new-found faith—even at the risk of being ridiculed or rejected. This woman whom I once loathed a couple decades before, I now found to be extraordinary in her kindness and humility.

Becky had become good friends with Jason and Laura, a couple in the Washington D.C. area who had recently left the Church. She suggested we all make the three hour drive and spend a weekend together. Jason was a returned missionary, and he and Laura got married in the temple. A crazy rainstorm came up out of nowhere shortly after we arrived at their house. It was so unlike anything we had seen back home in the desert. Dark, threatening clouds arose, swiftly moving across the sky, bringing with them lightening, booming thunder, and rain that looked like it was being thrown from buckets against the windows.

The weather was decent the following day, so we all went sight-seeing. We visited the Lincoln Memorial, the Washington Monument, and spent some time at the Smithsonian Institute. By mid-afternoon rain clouds gathered once again and began to downpour as we walked some distance back to the van. While most passers-by carried umbrellas or walked under awnings, the kids and I tromped out in the open in the falling rain. It rains so little in Las Vegas that this was an exciting event.

Over the weekend we watched hours of creation science videos from Jason's collection. I was astounded by the wealth of information available from Christian sources. As a Mormon I was pretty insulated from outside influences, preferring to spend my time and money on materials produced by the Church or by LDS teachers.

Our traveling schedule was coming to an end, and with warm but tearful good-byes to Becky, the boys and I packed our bags and headed to Utah, where our vacation would culminate in attending our family reunion. The whole trip was an thrilling adventure. We had the opportunity to visit a variety of churches: Baptist, Assemblies of God, Pentecostal, and non-denominational. The worship services were somewhat diverse, but they all had one thing in common; believers in Jesus Christ who honored and loved him. This was so different from the "bickering and contending" that my Mormon leaders said characterized Protestant denominations.

The year continued to usher in unexpected blessings. The rest of my family—who had stayed in Las Vegas—drove up to Utah so we could all rendezvous at the reunion. While there, we were invited to Dennis and Rauni Higley's house for dinner (best cooking west of the Rocky Mountains). This was the first time our children met them. They told the story of how they left Mormonism, while we all sat in rapt attention. Summer was visibly shaken, but wanted to know the truth once and for all. She asked Rauni to show her the evidences from official LDS sources, which Rauni was able to do. The last straw for my daughter was when she read Joseph Smith's boast:

> Come on! ye prosecutors! ye false swearers! All hell, boil over! Ye burning mountains, roll down your lava! for [sic] I will come out on the top at last. I have more to boast of than ever any man had. I am the only man that has ever been able to keep a whole church together since the days of Adam. A large majority of the whole have stood by me. Neither Paul, John, Peter, nor Jesus ever did it. I boast that no man ever did such a work as I. The followers of Jesus ran away from Him; but the Latter-day Saints never ran away from me yet.[2]

Summer previously thought that Joseph's alleged boast was made up by "anti-Mormons," but here it was in one of the volumes of Church History, along with his assurance that his words were accurately recorded;

You know my daily walk and conversation. I am in the bosom of a virtuous and good people. How I do love to hear the wolves howl! When they can get rid of me, the devil will also go. For the last three years I have a record of all my acts and proceedings, for I have kept several good, faithful, and efficient clerks in constant employ: they have accompanied me everywhere, and carefully kept my history, and they have written down what I have done, where I have been, and what I have said; therefore my enemies cannot charge me with any day, time, or place, but what I have written testimony to prove my actions; and my enemies cannot prove anything against me.[3]

Summer read Smith's whole speech, including the part where he denied having more than one wife. At the time of his denial in May of 1844, Smith had, in fact, over 30 documented wives. Summer snapped the book shut. "That does it for me," she said. By the time we all returned to our home in Las Vegas, we had only two believing Mormons in the family: Quinn and Jeff.

Quinn decided his best course of action was to admit himself to rehab. Money was a consideration. Almost all the programs available cost big bucks, which none of us had. However, the Salvation Army had a drug addiction treatment program. It required Quinn to live at their men's home twenty-four-seven. It was a strict program with mandatory schedules, expectations, responsibilities, and chapel attendance. They offered work-therapy, counseling, and spiritual direction, all free of charge. A few months later Quinn wrote home to say that he had come to know Jesus Christ as Lord and Savior, and that he finally understood Mormonism could not possibly be the true gospel or true Church.

As an aside, Quinn later had several opportunities to speak to teens at a youth detention center, warning them about the dangers of drugs, and telling them how a relationship with Jesus Christ could transform their lives.

Religious beliefs weren't the only changes in our family. By the time Jeff got home from his mission in February of 2004, Scott and I had divorced.

---

1. In an LDS Sacrament Meeting (the main worship service) several congregation members are assigned topics to give a "talk" on. The Bishop is unlike a pastor in that he doesn't preach. The "sermons" are called talks and are given by lay members.
2. *History of the Church, Volume 6*, pp. 408-409. Address of the Prophet—His Testimony Against the Dissenters at Nauvoo.
3. Ibid

CHAPTER 26

Tying Up Loose Ends

Neo, sooner or later you're going to realize just as I did that there's a difference between knowing the path and walking the path.

—Morpheus, The Matrix

Now you've come to the end of my story, at least insofar as my life as a Mormon goes. You may be wondering if I made mistakes after leaving the Church or what happened to our family. The answers may surprise you.

The transition from Mormonism to reality took its toll on our family, and while there were great joys and amazing discoveries, there were also challenges, obstacles, and uncertainties. I'd like to use the following analogy to provide some insight into what it feels like for people who leave Mormonism, especially those who believed it with their whole hearts and souls. I'm not asking you to agree that Mormonism isn't true; I'm asking if you can try to understand how someone might feel after coming to that conclusion.

Imagine going home to your parents' house to visit. You go in the attic to look for something, and while poking around you find a small chest with some papers in it. You examine the documents and learn, to your horror, that you were born the opposite sex. So, if you are now a man you learn you were born female, and if you are a woman you learn you were born male. You were born the opposite of what your parents wanted, so they arranged for a sex-change operation when you were still an infant. Everything that you had thought about yourself, others, and the world was built on a lie. All the time you were growing up you felt different and didn't know why. The way you looked at life was based on who you thought you were and what you believed was true.

If something like this happened, your world would crumble around you. You wouldn't know *what* to trust, let alone *whom* to trust. You would have to re-learn almost everything; the way you interacted with others, the way you dressed, and so much more, assuming you decided to return to the gender you were born as. Even if you stayed the artificial gender, there would be psychological ramifications. What if you had married? What if every major decision you made was based on what you thought was truth; that you were a man (or a woman)? There would be so much fallout your head would be spinning. Imagine the rage, despair, grief, sorrow, anguish, mistrust, and confusion you would feel.

This is the closest analogy I can think of to describe what people coming out of Mormonism go through. The longer they were members of the Church and the more they genuinely believed it to be true, the more severe their distress coming out of it. Someone who had been LDS all his or her life experiences greater tumult than someone who was a convert for only a year or two. However, even those who leave the Church after just a couple years experience a great sense of loss.

Obviously, the analogy only goes so far. In the story, the parents foisted the deception knowingly upon the child. In real life, members of the Church are not intentionally deceiving people. This analogy is meant only to illustrate the emotional devastation many Mormons experience when they believe they've been played for fools. I, for one, certainly felt several of the emotions described in the story; at first disbelief, followed by anger, then sorrow, loss, and a sense of purposelessness, depression, and finally—after a few years—healing.

When I was in that stage of anger at the Church, I wanted nothing to do with anything Mormonism stood for. I felt like a gazelle that was raised in captivity only to discover it was meant to be free. So, as soon as I cleared the fence I took off running. The upside was the truth that we are indeed meant to be free of manmade doctrines and institutional religiosity. There's nothing wrong with turning from such things. The downside is the danger of "throwing the baby out with the bathwater," which is what I did for a time.

If the Church taught modesty, I was going to dress any way I wanted to. If Mormon leaders told people not to drink, by golly I was going to enjoy a "brewski" (even if I didn't *really* enjoy it. Beer kind of tasted like corroded copper pennies in fizzy swamp-water). Delicious or not, I drank it anyway. The day after handing in my Church resignation letter, I bought a tea kettle, a coffee maker, a coffee bean grinder, and signed up for the Gevalia coffee club (and by the way, if you act now, you can get a programmable coffee maker for only $14.95 with shipping and handling).

Now, it's not that wearing a sleeveless shirt or having an occasional beer or drinking coffee is going to send someone to hell—it won't. But it was my attitude that was wrong. When I knew I would be around ward members (remember, at that point half of my family was still LDS), I made sure to wear a low-cut tank top with plenty of cleavage showing, and shorts barely covering my rear-end. To give you an idea of how I dressed, one time I took our van in for an oil change. By then I had gotten personalized license plates that read XLDS4JC. When I went to pay for the service, the manager came out and said, "You've gotta tell me about your license plates. I understand the 'Extra Large D's' (he said this while holding cupped hands out in front of his chest), but who is JC?"

All laughing aside though, I'd like to tell my LDS family, friends, and ward members who witnessed my disrespectful behavior that I'm sorry. I'm sorry for "strutting my stuff" in front of you as if your feelings and beliefs didn't matter. This isn't to say that ex-Mormons have to keep dressing like temple-recommend holders for the sake of appearances, but a person can still be modest in some sleeveless tops and shorts just above the knees. I pretty much went to an extreme.

Another mistake I made was throwing tact and sensitivity out the window. Just because *my* eyes had been opened and I was seeing things from a new perspective, I acted as if all it would take to open everyone else's eyes was some blunt truth. As a Mormon, one of the things people liked about me was that I just told things like they were. And I did. Whenever I bore my testimony in church, gave a Sacrament Meeting talk, or taught a Sunday school or Relief Society lesson I pretty much shot straight from the hip. I'd give encouragement where it was needed, admonishment when necessary, and always looked to the teachings of LDS prophets past and present to have the courage to speak the unpopular.

As an example, it wasn't popular to tell priesthood holders that they should work two jobs if necessary so their wives could stay home to raise the children. It wasn't popular to tell the sisters who wanted to work that their calling was to be wives and mothers, not breadwinners. Why? Because that's what Church leaders taught for well over a century; and if it came from *their* lips it was the same as coming from the mouth of Heavenly Father. Thus, I had acquired a reputation as "Tell-it-like-it-is-Tracy." It may have irritated the heck out of a few people, but for the most part I received pats on the back for it.

Now the tables were turned. My propensity to "tell it like it is" drove a wedge between me and others after I left the Church.

Instead of saying something like this;

> **Respectful, tactful:** "In my research from the Church's genealogical records, I found that 11 of Joseph Smith's wives were married to other men at the time."

I said something more like this;

> **Disrespectful, not so tactful:** "You'll never believe what I found out! Old Joe was schtooping other men's wives!"

Instead of saying this;

> **Kind, diplomatic:** "It's imperative for people to know who God is and to understand Jesus as he presents himself in the Bible, or else they may face eternal consequences."

I said something more or less like this,

> **Unkind, shocking:** "Yep, Mormons are going to hell."

I know this is probably too little, too late, but I want to apologize to my family members and friends who were appalled and hurt by my insensitivity. I'm sorry I didn't take your feelings into consideration and spoke so disrespectfully to you about things you considered sacred. While I don't believe we shouldn't speak openly and candidly about things that concern or trouble us, our speech should "always be gracious and interesting, so that [we] will know how to respond to any particular individual" (Colossians 4:6, CJB). I stepped over the line on many occasions, and I want to take this opportunity to tell you I'm truly sorry for the times I was obnoxious, sarcastic, and cavalier in my words and actions.

My Marriage

Three years after leaving Mormonism Scott and I divorced. It was *not* because we left the Church. Although Scott has encouraged me all along to just "tell it like it is," it's unnecessary to provide details. The truth is that despite his faults and actions I felt I couldn't live with any more—truly believing they were affecting the well-being of the family—he is an amazing person and my children's father. Besides that, I admit I certainly was not Little Miss Perfect myself. We were both doing the best we could under the circumstances we were in over the years. Divorce may be justifiable in some cases, but it is nonetheless a serious and sad event. I'm happy to report that we remain good friends to this very day and only wish the very best for each other.

A year after my divorce, I met a Christian man and remarried. Scott says he "doesn't think of it as losing a wife as much as gaining a husband-in-law." My husband doesn't quite think of it that way, but that's okay. He graciously allows Scott in our lives and in our home for the sake of the kids. All is well.

To this day, all manner of rumors continue to be spread and perpetuated by the ill-informed and, frankly, if I may say so, the ignorant. I've heard a lot of unkind and untrue things through the grapevine about why we left the Church; everything from me running off with some guy and abandoning my kids, to Scott and me being "swingers" (partner swapping). Come on, people! Get real. Does embracing those rumors strengthen your belief that the Church is true? Is your testimony so fragile that it has to be bolstered up by believing the worst about those who leave? Why is it so hard for some Mormons to just accept the fact that someone can leave the Church for intellectually and spiritually honest reasons?

You've read my account, and while you might not agree with my conclusions, please have the decency and courtesy to take it at face value. I left Mormonism for nothing less and nothing more than the reasons given in this book. If you have questions, feel free to ask me directly rather than passing on unsubstantiated gossip. We can have reasonable and civil discussions, can we not?

I have a great deal of respect for one of my LDS nephews who had the courage to ask me if a certain rumor was true. It was not. We had a wonderful conversation that lasted several hours and have become very close because of it. You're an amazing young man, Isaac. Thank you for your love and support.

My Family

As of this third printing, one of my ten children remains devout LDS. Tragically, in many families where someone leaves the Church while others remain loyal to Mormonism, religious differences damage or destroy relationships. We've been very blessed that this didn't happen to us. We've all made an effort to listen to each other and allow one another to express our dearly-held beliefs, even though they may differ from our own. We value each other, our relationships, and our family unity. Our love is stronger than our individual desires to prove one another wrong. We can address religious issues openly and freely because we're secure in the knowledge that our differences have no bearing on the love we have for one another. By the grace of God we remain a close-knit family.

Conclusion

Now we've come full-circle. Instead of choosing to keep my blinders on, which the Apostle Peter called being "willfully ignorant" (2 Peter 3:5), I took the "red pill" and dove into the rabbit hole to see how deep it went. My journey took me through Wonderland after disconnecting from the Matrix of Mormonism. I discovered amazing and compelling things in the Bible about the God of Abraham, Isaac, and Jacob—things that are both wondrous and sobering. In my study of history and the Bible in recent years, I came to learn that Jesus—Yeshua—was thoroughly Jewish in every way. He was not the prototype Mormon. He wore a tallit (prayer shawl worn during morning prayers, on Shabbat, and holidays), taught in the synagogues, wore a phylactery (tefillin),[1] kept the seventh-day Sabbath, participated in all the Jewish feasts and festivals, and was a respected rabbi.

The 1st Century church was a sect of Judaism up until around the second century CE. Christianity didn't completely break away until the time of the Roman Emperor Constantine, although it underwent a gradual separation prior to his conversion. The more one studies Jewish and Church history, the more obvious it becomes that Mormonism is not the "restoration of the gospel." The Mormon gospel and the Messianic gospel of Jesus and his disciples have very little in common. Mormonism can claim to be a *new revelation* of the gospel, but not a *restoration*.

For instance, the Jewish temple was a house of sacrifices of various types; not a place where "worthy members" went to have ordinances performed for themselves and in behalf of the dead. Marriages were celebrated by the whole community of faith, in public view; not behind closed doors in secret, with unfortunate "non-members" being excluded. The Aaronic priesthood detailed in the Torah doesn't even resemble the Aaronic priesthood of Mormonism.

The exciting news is that those who diligently seek God will find Him (Proverbs 8:17). This proverb proved to be true for me. I had to set aside my fears and preconceptions and tell the God of Abraham, Isaac, and Jacob with all earnestness of heart that I wanted to know Him and His truth, even if it meant I had been wrong all my life. God was faithful. He brought me out of the kingdom of darkness into His marvelous light. I'm not Mormon, evangelical, Protestant, Catholic, or any other label. I prefer to simply be called a follower of Jesus and child of the Most High.

I have no regrets leaving The Church of Jesus Christ of Latter-day Saints. I found Life—the abundant life—in Yeshua of Nazareth, promised Messiah, resurrected on the third day, and returning at the end of the age. May you, too, diligently seek Him and find Him.

---

1. Teffilin, also known as phylacteries, are used to literally bind God's word to a person's hand and forehead. "Traditional Jews keep this commandment by strapping leather boxes (teffilin) containing relevant passages of Scripture to their hands and foreheads during morning prayer. This ancient custom was universal among the mainstream of observant Jews of Yeshua's day. He almost certainly practiced the custom" (D. Thomas Lancaster, *Restoration: Returning the Torah of God to the Disciples of Jesus.* Marshfield: First Fruits of Zion, 2011), 106.

OPRAH

THE OPRAH WINFREY SHOW

March 2, 2000

Tracy Crookston
▮▮▮▮▮▮▮▮▮▮▮▮▮▮
Las Vegas, NV 89130

Dear Tracy,

Thank you for being a guest on the show.

We appreciate your taking time to share yourself with our
viewers and studio audience.

Sincerely,

Oprah Winfrey

OW/jjb

110 N. CARPENTER
CHICAGO ILLINOIS

Appendix

Changes in the Mormon Church since 2018

- Missionaries are allowed to call home once a week instead of only twice a year (previously Mother's Day and Christmas).

- Sister missionaries are now allowed to wear pants in most missions, but not to church.

- Sunday meetings have been reduced from the three-hour block schedule to two hours.

- Relief Society and priesthood meetings are now held two Sundays each month (instead of weekly), with Sunday school on alternate Sundays.

- The home-teaching and visiting-teaching programs have been renamed "ministering." It is essentially the same as before, only reporting is quarterly instead of monthly, and there is more flexibility in the message or lesson taught. The visits are now called "interviews." Young women age 14 and older can now participate as "ministers.," whereas before only young men could.

- Boys will be able to be ordained to the Aaronic priesthood and pass the Sacrament (communion) during Sacrament Meeting at the beginning of the calendar year in which they turn 12, instead of waiting until their birthday.

- Couples can now be sealed in the temple immediately after a civil wedding ceremony instead of having to wait one year. This was already allowed in many countries outside of the United States.

- Changes in the temple ceremony include shorter sessions, wording of covenants and vows making them more female-friendly, and a new movie that is comprised of still-shots and narration instead of full live-action acting.

- The Church severed its long-standing relationship with the Boy Scouts of America and is introducing its own youth program.

- The First Presidency issued a statement declaring that members are no longer to refer to themselves or the Church as Mormon or Latter-day Saint, but to use the Church's full name.

Resources

Recommended Books on Real Mormon History

One Nation Under Gods: A History of the Mormon Church, Richard Abanes (Basic Books, 2003)

Mormon America: The Power and the Promise, Richard and Joan Ostling (Harper-Collins, 2009)

In Sacred Lonliness: The Plural Wives of Joseph Smith, Todd M. Compton (Signature Books, 1997)

The Mormon Hierarchy: Origins of Power, D. Michael Quinn (Signature Books, 1994)

Mormonism: Shadow or Reality, Jerald and Sandra Tanner (Utah Lighthouse Ministry, 1987)

("Mormonism: Shadow or Reality" is a comprehensive, well-documented, and insightful resource.)

Recommended Websites

Utah Lighthouse Ministry: utlm.org

H.I.S. Ministries International: hismin.com

Equipping Christians Ministries: equippingchristians.com

Institute for Religious Research: mit.irr.org

Ex-Mormon Files: exmormonfiles.com

Recommended Books on Judeo-Christian History and Apologetics

Sitting at the Feet of Rabbi Jesus, Ann Spangler and Lois Tverberg (Zondervan, 2009)

Our Father Abraham: Jewish Roots of the Christian Faith, Marvin J. Wilson (Eerdmans Publishing, 1989)

Cold Case Christianity, J. Warner Wallace (David C. Cook Publishing, 2013)

Author can be contacted at: TracyTennant@Outlook.com

Other Books by Tracy Tennant

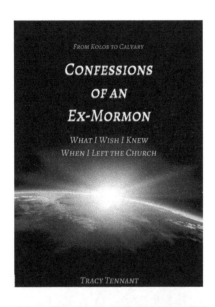

Available through online bookstores!

Printed in the USA
CPSIA information can be obtained
at www.ICGtesting.com
LVHW010225141223
766485LV00012B/595